Barns

Randy Leffingwell

MBI Publishing Company

DEDICATION

For Carolyn.
Next time, you come along.

First published in 2001 by MBI Publishing Company, Galtier Plaza, Suite 200, 380 Jackson Street, St. Paul, MN 55101-3885 USA

MBI Publishing Company books are also available at discounts in bulk quantity for industrial or sales-promotional use. For details write to Special Sales Manager at Motorbooks International Wholesalers & Distributors, Galtier Plaza, Suite 200, 380 Jackson Street, St. Paul, MN 55101-3885 USA.

Edited by Darwin Holmstrom
Designed by Arthur Durkee

Library of Congress Cataloging-in-Publication Data
    Barns/Randy Leffingwell.
        p. cm.—(Enthusiast color series)
    Includes index.
    ISBN 0-7603-1151-X (pbk.: alk. paper)
        1. Barns—United States—Pictorial works.
    2. Vernacular architecture—United States—Pictorial works. I. Title. II. Series.
    NA8230.L453   2001
    728'.922'0973—dc21   2001030732

On the front cover: Gambrel-roof, banked dairy barn, Rentschler farm, Saline, Michigan
This barn's simple gambrel roof is framed with rain gutters. This is a far less costly alternative to the "tilted plate" construction that adds a roof kick-up to deflect rain and snow out farther from the walls, preserving the foundation. Storage for wagons and hay (and later tractors and harvesters) was above the stone foundation which surrounded the dairy milking parlor.

On the frontispiece: This barn, built in 1913, contains a 143-foot front milking parlor, bisected by this doorway. The C-shaped barn has 6,128 glass windows.

On the title page: This classic gambrel-roofed barn is on the Greenland Ranch near Larkspur, Colorado.

On the back cover: This 1,000-acre farm was formerly owned by Albert Fancher, a New York state senator.

Printed in China

CONTENTS

ACKNOWLEDGMENTS

A number of historic sites and living history museums allowed me access to shoot and research. I am grateful to the Central Coast Lighthouse Keepers Association, Point Sur, California; Frank Lloyd Wright Foundation, Taliesin West, Scottsdale, Arizona; Hancock Shaker Village, Hancock, Massachusetts; Historic St. Mary's City, St. Mary's, Maryland; Plimoth Plantation, Plymouth, Massachusetts; Taliesin Preservation Commission, Spring Green, Wisconsin; Vermont Farm Bureau, Richmond, Vermont; and Yorktown Victory Center, Yorktown, Virginia.

I owe much thanks to many individuals for their help: William B. Armstrong, Harrington, Washington; Helen and Nunce Cina, Viroqua, Wisconsin; Allison Clark, Denver, North Carolina; Marciel and Mel Cronrath, Harrington, Washington; Dorothy Ellis, Springfield Township, Michigan; Guy Fay, Madison, Wisconsin; Larry and Wendy Friesen, Altona, Manitoba, Canada; Ron and Marilyn Hamm, Altona, Manitoba, Canada; Erik Henriksson, New Dungeness Chapter, U.S. Lighthouse Society; Professor Thomas C. Hubka, School of Architecture and Urban Planning, University of Wisconsin, Milwaukee, Wisconsin; David B. Kaufman, Oley, Pennsylvania; Patricia Kellogg, Kamloops, British Columbia, Canada; Duncan Keir, Liberty Head Post & Beam, Huntington, Vermont; Vernon Kline and family, Shreve, Ohio; Bob Lang, Waitsfield, Vermont; Alberta Lewallan, Linden, California; Ralph and Ruth Odenkirk, Orrville, Ohio; Herman and Donna Ostry, Bruno, Nebraska; Alice Outback, Waitsfield, Vermont; Wayne and Edith Patenaude, East St. Johnsbury, Vermont; Albert and Madeline Petramala, Pinon Heights, Colorado; Jerald and Madolyn Redman, McComb, Illinois; Clyde, Mary, and Craig Rust, Davis, California; Tony and Kay Schimpf, DX Ranch, Knutsford, British Columbia, Canada; Kim and Greg Seefert, Marine on St. Croix, Minnesota; John Skolfield, Winter Park, Florida; The Honorable Helen Marie Taylor, Orange, Virginia; Mrs. Aldine Valent, and Jim and Frank Valent, Salamanca, New York; Ruth Wheeler, Hardwick, Massachusetts; Gil and David White, St. John, Washington; and Sarah Williamson, Huntington Center, Vermont.

I am ever grateful to Lorry Dunning, historical consultant, Davis, California, for his thoughtful suggestions throughout this project.

Finally, I want to thank Darwin Holmstrom, my editor at MBI Publishing Company, for proposing this book and going without sleep to make it happen.

—*Randy Leffingwell*
Ojai, California

INTRODUCTION

Everyone who has driven down a country lane can recall seeing barns teetering precariously or even collapsed into messes of gray wood. Yet for each of those, there are 10 or 100 others still standing, still at work. It is those barns, built throughout the continent from the dreams and ambitions of millions of farmers that fill this book.

Previous page
Preservation or abandonment, near Fargo, North Dakota
Barn preservation is challenged by a double-edged sword in the United States. Barns represent an investment, an asset, yet maintaining them is costly. Repairing or painting them can increase property taxes because the improvements increase the value of the farm. Modern machinery barely fits through doorways meant for horse-drawn wagons, causing many farmers to watch as weather and age defeat their structures.

As European immigrants settled in the New World, they encountered problems and challenges that demanded modifications to the barn traditions they had carried with them. From their adaptations came American barns.

Local conditions and building materials greatly influenced these adaptations. Wood was abundant in the Northeast, but more scarce in other regions. In Pennsylvania and Wisconsin where limestone and other rock could be readily quarried builders adopted stone as a construction material. Scarce water and fierce winter winds dictated the shapes of barns in the West. All across the continent, local factors such as these reconfigured the barns built by migrants.

In the early 1800s, mill-sawn lumber standardized timber dimensions, introducing the first hint of sameness to barns and buildings. Transplanted Connecticut carpenter Augustine Taylor inadvertently accelerated this homogenization when he built a church in Chicago in 1830 using slender wall studs rather than traditional timber frame construction. By the late 1800s, his carpenter's adaptation had led to the nationwide dispersal of precut, ready-to-assemble, nearly identical kit barns purchased from Midwest mail-order catalogs like that offered by Sears Roebuck. Mass production spread out like spokes of a wheel, and carried the styles of barns and their construction from catalog offices in Chicago and lumberyards in St. Louis. What had been visions in imaginations became full-color illustrations with catalog numbers. Cut it out, fold it up, and carry it in a billfold.

Farm journals also contributed to more standardized barns. As writers learned of new concepts or techniques, they wrote about and illustrated what other farmers, builders, or regions had to offer. This information spread to a population of farmers hungry to succeed and anxious to learn.

By the early 1900s many of America's earliest barns had been outgrown or were beginning to fail and were ready for replacement. A near frenzy of building followed a virtual barn renaissance.

Today's farming business has little use for tradition and heritage. There is too much money at stake and too little profit returned. Reconfiguring a healthy barn or saving one at peril can be more costly than removing it and building a new steel structure. Still, barns are preserved. Fortunately for barn enthusiasts and historians, there are farmers who are willing to ignore profitability in the interest of tradition and heritage. What they preserve may be their own family tradition or ethnic culture, but the act of barn salvation transcends a single family to embrace the entire community and provide a link to our country's heritage.

Gambrel-roof yard sheds, Lancaster, Pennsylvania
At farm and ranch supply outlets around the United States, a number of manufacturers sell barn-like structures to house lawn and garden furniture, lawn mowers, and bicycles while reminding us of our agrarian roots. Without ongoing commitment to preserve existing barns, these may become the only barns standing.

CHAPTER I

THE ORIGIN OF AMERICAN BARNS

America's earliest settlers expected riches equal to the gold shipped back to Spain by Spanish explorers. Instead, they found starvation and privation. Their situation remained grim until the establishment of a cash crop that ultimately reversed their fortunes. Smoking tobacco saved the New World from economic failure and brought the first need for barns to America.

Hayrick, Plimoth Plantation, Plymouth, Massachusetts
At Massachusetts Bay Colony, settlers erected simple structures on a scale that made sense. This 1620s-era 11x11-foot hayrick adapted English thatched roof techniques to hard colonial winters, allowing stalls for two cows below the hay.

The thatched roof was a typical English and northern European construction. Builders accommodated changing hay stocks with a roof height that allowed as much as 7 feet of adjustment. The nearly 3-foot overhang kept rain and snow off the cattle feed.

By the late 1620s pigs and cows brought over from England joined corn and beans as foodstuffs for the colonists. Farmers quickly learned that letting the livestock forage freely in the forests fattened them suitably. Southern farmers learned that their New World seacoast suffered winters mild enough that none of their animals needed to be sheltered even in the coldest months. Such buildings as existed were constructed to keep corn and tobacco dry. This was not the case in Massachusetts, however, where the long frost season started in November and lingered until April. Livestock had to be housed and fed for four to six months.

The barns that immigrated to the New World were large, substantial buildings. The earliest English barns, built in the 1100s, were essentially warehouses meant for storing the grains grown on vast estates. The huge stone barns, some more than 40 feet wide and over 140 feet long, were built with steeply pitched roofs (supported by elaborate hewn-timber frames) to shed frequent rainfalls. Stone posts and spines provided the large, uncluttered interior spaces needed to store grain. These grain and livestock storage buildings provided the mental pictures that most settlers carried to America.

The first New England versions were small, described as one-, two-, or three-bay barns. Each bay served a purpose and each was defined by a bent, the assemblage of various posts and beams that made up the internal structure of the barn. English barns were always entered through doors in the center of the long sidewall, never from the gable end. The doors were placed on both sides of the building. While this symmetry was pleasing to the eye it was also functional. Oxen or horses drew a cart or wagon into the barn to be unloaded into one side bay or the other. The horses then walked straight out the other side. Barns were situated so that prevailing winds would pass through the open doors (and up and over the peak, rather than smashing into the tall, vertical, gable end). Threshing took advantage of the winds blowing through the building to carry away the lighter chaff while the grain fell to the floor. Farmers then shoveled the grain into bins in the bay opposite the unthreshed grain.

Builders used whatever wood was available locally to frame their barns. In the earliest cases in the colonies, they used entire timbers, resulting in structures that looked like log cabins. Later they flattened the sides of the logs with broadaxes. Logs that had been given one, two, or four flat sides were called hewn timbers. During the eighteenth century when lumber mills were established, timbers squared up by

English-style tobacco barn, Historic St. Mary's City, St. Mary's, Maryland
Early colonial settlers' most valuable crop was tobacco and this 20x40-foot Sussex, England-style barn, one of two at this living history farm, demonstrates how 50 to 75 years of colonial success had increased crop yield. This 1700s-era structure was built directly on the ground with no foundation. Vertical beams planted in dirt provided support.

English tobacco barn, Yorktown Victory Center, Yorktown, Virginia
This simple 16x20-foot post-and-beam structure is described as a 1780s-era "eight-room" tobacco barn. Based on typical Suffolk-region, English-style barns with a center front door, the open interior space allows for drying eight sets of 4-foot-long tobacco shafts. Tobacco plants grow in the foreground.

English-style barn, Kline farm, Shreve, Ohio

Guarding their traditions carefully, the Amish still turn out to build a barn in a day. The 16-foot-tall back wall of a 40x40-foot haymow goes up here. Workers wait on upper horizontal "end girts" to pound oak pegs into the rising rear "plate" at the top.

large radial saw blades were called sawn or milled. Broadaxed or hewn wood is easily recognized by the repetitive but slightly irregular chop marks along the length of the timber and typically perpendicular to it. The wood finish was usually surprisingly smooth but just slightly uneven. Sawn or milled timber was regular and square at the four corners and the regular cuts of the long pit or whip saw or of the rotating saw blade was recognizable.

Barns in New England were built on foundations of fieldstone laid on leveled ground, much as barns were constructed in England. Sometimes a mortar was made of a kind of limestone slurry but as often as not, gravity and the weight of the timber structure above it held the barn and foundation to the

ground. The dimensions of the barn were determined not only by the size of the farm but also by the trees available of matching lengths. The entire structure usually rested on a sill that effectively accepted whatever moisture crept up the stone foundation from the ground. Each bent, set on top of the sill, was connected to the next by horizontal beams around the perimeter called girts and by massive, load-bearing beams through the middle called summer beams.

Girts and summer beams provided stability and support midway up the barn structure. At the top, the girts were called plates while summer beams were simply labeled second summer beams. Obviously, front and rear girts and plates and summer beams had to be the same length and

English dairy barn
Not quite 10 hours after raising the first wall, Amish workers finish nailing roof panels in place while others begin clean up on the ground. The 92-foot-wide structure is 40 feet deep with a milking parlor below (through the cattle door, lower left.

While there is no electricity, this Amish farmer powers his milking machine with a small diesel engine started on its own battery. The concrete walls and floors of this milking parlor ensure sanitary conditions and make clean up after milking easier.

barns of pleasing symmetry required that the three bays be of nearly equal dimension. Therefore, a three-bay barn required dozens of timbers of matched lengths. What's more, because of the loads, these plates sometimes measured as long as 22 feet, though some individual beams stretched more than 60 or 70 feet. But the more-or-less standard length was 16 to 16.5 feet, a rod in classical measurement. In truth, the lengths varied between 14 and 17 feet. Therefore a three-bay barn was usually 42 to 51 feet long and one-half to two-thirds that in width.

However, the earliest barns in the New World were nowhere near so grand. One-bay structures more accurately represent the scale of farming in the earliest days of the New World. The hay barn at Plimoth Plantation, an early seventeenth-century living history museum south of Boston, Massachusetts, is 11 feet square.

At Yorktown Victory Center, an eighteenth-century living history museum near Colonial Williamsburg, where the cash crop was tobacco, 11x11-inch corner posts and 8x8-inch center posts support a replica 16x20-foot barn. The barn is divided not into bays but into rooms, areas 4 or 5 feet wide that run the length or width of the barn. Each room is divided further by horizontal tiers (pronounced "tires"), which support the tobacco hanging on 4- or 5-foot-long sticks to dry. A barn this size would hold about 4,000 pounds of tobacco and the drying process would take four to six weeks in the early fall. Both the Plimoth and Yorktown barns were loosely sided to allow air to flow in and out of the structure to dry the tobacco, grain, or hay.

Each of these barns was constructed without foundations, with their corner posts planted into the ground in a manner called earthfast. This was a construction technique that offered ease, simplicity, and quickness as its major benefits. But ground moisture would begin the deterioration process very soon unless chestnut, locust, or cedar was used for the downposts. In the early days of the New World, however, this was neither a problem nor a worry. Tobacco

Hay bales are stacked to the rafters through the fall to provide feed for the herd throughout the winter. The open slats at the end of the gables allow for the hay to dry more efficiently. Built of fresh green oak and covered with 1x12 pine boards, the barn required 40,000 board feet of lumber.

used up the land within five years, and new fields were constantly opened, so it was often easier to build a new tobacco barn at the new fields than to repair and relocate the old one. And in New England, the scale of farming grew rapidly and its emphasis changed frequently so that the sizes and configurations of many barns were obsolete even before the downposts rotted. Where in the 1620s a wealthy farmer had two cows, in the 1660s, families may have had a dozen, and the new barn needed to hold winter feed and the 12 cows. With more time to plan than was available for the hurried first barn construction, sills and stone foundations could be carefully prepared. The farmer moved and then sold his old, inadequate earthfast farmstead to the next arrival off the boat. And the process would begin again.

An interesting opportunity to see this kind of development exists at Historic St. Mary's City, the first capital of Maryland. Two nearly identical barns are reconstructed there about 50 yards apart. They are both the same size—roughly 20x40 feet—but the one father from the road is incorporated into a setting that replicates a mid-seventeenth-century farmstead with a two-story house nearby. It is constructed of white oak, erected in a series of bents that were built earthfast, the vertical posts of which were sunk directly into the ground without benefit of sills or foundation. Five-foot long white oak clapboards are nailed horizontally onto the downposts. This typifies the style of barn built by immigrant English carpenters working in the easiest, quickest, and cheapest manner. The barn nearer to the road re-creates the work of an early eighteenth-century carpenter with the same needs: the creation of an easy, quick, and inexpensive structure.

The later barn, also built of white oak, is assembled not in bents but by what's known as sidewall construction. The front wall is raised, then the back, and then collars are lifted up and dropped in to tie the whole thing together.

The expansion of farming and of landholdings caused the rapid building of new barns in New England. With the death of communal farming came the end of common grazing grounds in the centers of the towns and villages. Those owners with land grants farther out from the common often sold or traded their land to farmers closer in who needed to expand their operations. Small barns ringed the commons but the annual outward expansion brought a frequency of new, larger building or of existing buildings enlarged.

It wasn't just the scale of the land but also the wealth of trees that astonished colonists in the New World. In England, which had been at war with one country or another for nearly 600 years, the last tall straight trees that hadn't been used in the building of castles, manors, or churches were consumed building sailing ships. After the battles with the Spanish Armada in 1522, crown soldiers traveled throughout all England marking as the King's own property any tree taller than 16 feet. These were meant for use as masts and spars for warships.

To arrive in Massachusetts and find white pines reaching 150 to 200 feet straight up—and to find them stretching as far as one could see—staggered the first builders. It scarcely mattered that the English Navy had laid claim to any colonial white pine with a trunk diameter greater than 2 feet across; that still left the settlers with 100 million other trees with which to build.

And build they did.

New England-style dairy barn, Wheeler farm, Hardwick, Massachusetts

Built in 1890 with its entry on the end, not the side, this 75-foot-long, 27-foot-tall barn was enlarged in the 1940s, extending its length another 31 feet when Bill and Ruth Wheeler expanded their dairy herd from 38 to 50 cows. But like many old barns, as this upper window shows, things sag.

By the early 1800s, American builders had moved the entrance to the end of English-style barns. They simplified techniques too, using angled "queen" posts to open more hay storage space inside and support a lighter, simpler roof structure.

CHAPTER 2

THE INFLUENCE OF NORTHERN EUROPE

E ven as immigration continued, migration began. The population of America was growing rapidly. New lands were needed for farms and villages because of the steady arrival of settlers not only from England but also from northern and central European countries as well.

Swiss-style barn, Michael Schryner farm, Oregon, Pennsylvania
Michael Schryner built this forebay, or overhanging barn in 1828 on land granted to his father by Pennsylvania colonial governor William Penn in 1738. These Swiss-style barns utilized an overhang in the upper haymow that protected cattle from weather and allowed farmers to shovel feed through trap doors to the livestock below.

Swiss-style barn, Hoober-Eby farm, Neffsville, Pennsylvania
John Eby built this stylish barn in Lancaster County in 1860. German and Swiss farmer immigrants brought with them architectural styles including the habit of "decorating" front walls of the overhanging "Vorbau," or forebay, with louvers and window glass.

Farmers from the Netherlands brought with them a particular heritage that consolidated agriculture, animal husbandry, and their own home into a single structure. In the Old World, this rectangular building was known as a loshoe, with one large double doorway at one gable end. Unlike English barns that made no accommodation for sheltering livestock, the Dutch drove their animals into the barn through that doorway each night and back out each morning. Pigs lived nearest the door, with stalls for horses, cows and calves, and sheep lining the central aisle and leading away from the door. Animals faced into the center to facilitate feeding, and sometimes the ground level on which they stood was lower than the central aisle and even banked away from it. The

central aisle also served as a threshing floor. The gable-end doors provided access for wagons.

Two-thirds of the loshoe was home to the livestock and crops and it was built on a simple pounded dirt floor. The last third, farthest from the main door and insulated from winter cold by the heat of the animals, was the family home. A doorway on each side of the barn allowed access from the living quarters to the yards.

The residential area, generally built on a floor of cobblestones, comprised several rooms. Tiny sleeping chambers—closet sized, really—featured doors to provide some privacy to the sleepers and some further insulation from the weather and the odors. There were public areas, a kind of living room/dining area, and another room set aside for such activities as weaving. Cooking was done around an open hearth in the center of the floor very near the sleeping rooms. The family entertained visitors in a room near the hearth called the "best room," the finest room in the house. Above all of this the hayloft often extended the full length of the barn, further insulating the inhabitants and providing sleeping quarters for children and servants.

Builders constructed walls of wattle, a kind of intertwined weaving of sticks and twigs, and daub, a sort of clay plaster that forms a stucco to seal and strengthen the wattle. Thatch covered the barn's steeply-pitched—and usually hipped—roof.

Builders almost always constructed the barn/home around a well and the hearth was placed as close to it as possible. In the Netherlands, farmers burned peat in their hearth; it provided enough heat for cooking and winter warming. In the New World, the Dutch learned that peat was unavailable. They also found that Eastern winters were much harsher than the cold months in Holland. Wood fires burned hotter than peat fires, so the Dutch quickly adapted. Because of the threat of fire, they separated their homes from the barns. The rectangular loshoe became a nearly square barn once the residence was removed. Locating thatch proved to be a challenge in some northern areas so builders covered roofs with wood shingles. These New York and New Jersey farmers retained the big door in a gable end. However, they added another one at the opposite end (that was no longer blocked by living quarters). This eliminated the need to back the horses and wagon out after unloading the hay.

Forebay barns, Kaufman farm, Oley, Pennsylvania
These late 1800s Berks County, Pennsylvania Dutch-style barns were built in the "pielereck" forebay style, using stone gable walls extending to the ground for additional structural support and for weather protection for the livestock. This sheep barn is 33x40.

The stone walls are 20 inches thick in this cattle barn and in the sheep barn in front of it. This "pielereck" forebay barn offers only a 3-foot overhang while other Swiss- and German-style barns, oddly without the extra support of these side walls, stretch as much as 10 feet overhead.

Within the next century, the Dutch made another improvement on their barns. Still feeding and tending livestock off the central aisle, inventive builders considered the desirability of animal doors at the sides of the gable ends, just inside the eaves. As sizes of herds increased to such an extent that all the cows could not be milked at once, these livestock doors were added to both ends, just as the wagon doors had been. This allowed the animals to enter and exit the barn in one direction, without doubling back on incoming livestock.

The earliest German immigrants—called the Pennsylvania Dutch because the English mistook Duetsche, which means "German," for "Dutch"—began to arrive in the New World in the late 1600s. Their first simple structures were built of logs from the hardwood trees growing all around them. They notched these logs at the ends in order to secure one log on top of and perpendicular to the next. Spaces between the logs were often left open to allow air to dry the

harvest. Within a short time, however, the builders began to finish the logs on top and bottom for a closer fit; later they filled in the chinks between the logs to close up the barn against winter cold.

Family growth and continuing immigration swelled the German population, making more workers available to perform hand labor. Saw pits—in operation throughout Europe from the early 1600s—were established in the colonies, and the felled trees could be flattened on four sides. Elaborate notches and joinery were introduced to better and more tightly assemble and tie together the ever-growing barns.

When the great surges of Germanic colonists arrived during the first half of the 1700s, they found meadows laced with streams. They built structures familiar to them as their English neighbors had done a century before. Tall-roofed rectangular buildings appeared. But these differed from the Massachusetts barns and houses by the addition of a projection, a forebay, above the ground floor that was cantilevered out over the stockyard, providing more floor space up in the haymow.

Throughout middle Europe, in the crowded, walled towns in Britain, France, Switzerland, and Germany, this extension of the second floor expanded the living space of narrow, vertical houses in the only way possible: forward, out over the streets.

Most of the new settlers arriving from southern Germany and Switzerland were familiar with the idea of a "bank" structure. These people had stored hay and grain in banked barns, but they also lived in houses and worshiped in churches and paid their taxes in buildings built out from hillsides.

These German and Swiss farmers, like the English ahead of them, built what they knew. They adopted Pennsylvania natural resources—and probably some English ideas—where they needed to do so. Throughout Switzerland and Bavaria, the barns were built perpendicular to the slope of the hill, that is, out from the hill. In many of them, entry was from the gable end; fewer it seemed, were entered from the long side. In Pennsylvania, right from the start, barns were set on the site to run along the hill and entry was on the sidewall.

Log barns were usually made up of two squares of log bays that flanked an open loft between them. Very few log barns still exist anywhere in the eastern United States. The initial log barns were usually replaced by larger stone barns. The log structures slipped into secondary importance and finally into neglect.

Swiss barn ventilators, Little Spring Farm, Reinholds, Pennsylvania
There are as many styles of ventilation holes as there were nationalities building barns in the colonies. From narrow slits in stone work, to wood siding nailed an inch apart, to these patterns in the bricks on this 1870s barn, to elaborate louvers and opening glass windows, the purpose was the same. Air had to get inside the barn to dry the fresh hay to make usable feed.

Farms arose and grew rich as crops flourished and an agricultural marketplace developed in proximity to Philadelphia, encouraging farmers to enlarge their operations. Bigger barns were needed to accommodate greater crops and to hold them until market prices seemed best. Granaries and threshing floors had to be enlarged. Farmers recognized that livestock that was fed and stabled grew more quickly and predictably than cattle that ranged freely and foraged for their food. The evolution from farming with oxen to using horses meant that farmers had to keep oats and other grains for feed in addition to hay.

The labor pool grew, and workers for hire were now available. More agricultural equipment and more livestock— and stabling and pens—were required. Bigger, more demanding construction could be undertaken. These were works requiring larger, more massive timbers. They utilized stout internal structures to support heavier loads inside and carry bigger roofs over them.

The Pennsylvania Dutch settlers moved out in search of more lands, taking their Germanic ideas and designs with them. As with the English structures, the heavy but precisely measured framework of fitted and pegged timbers provided

27

Potato barn, Jost farm, Sagaponack, New York
Potato barns were an adaptation of the English bank barn. Instead of being constructed off a hillside, these were built into the ground to protect potatoes from freezing during the winter before the crop sold in the spring.

the structural support in German barns. But the new geography—or more accurately geology—that met the westward migrants crossing Pennsylvania, offered to them an even more permanent building material to supplement the timber.

End walls were soon built of quarried limestone laid up in a lime mortar. Barns constructed with the cantilevered forebay with sidewalls of stone have become known as "Sweitzer," or "Swisser," barns.

German builders generally constructed their barns with stone masonry up to the hayloft floor—even in structures where the rest of the primary construction was timber frame.

The heaviest hardwood timber was usually oak and often the pegs were too, although hickory or even maple or ash was used for pegs in some instances. The heavy flooring planks were most often oak as well. Wood siding, both of the exterior and of the boards set tightly about the granary space and defining the stalls, was usually pine; pine or spruce was generally selected for some of the smaller braces. Sawn timbers

were used only for lighter pieces of barn structure. The most massive pegged timbers of the structure were still formed by the ax and adze up to a decade or so before the Civil War.

Local fieldstone was used for each barn. As with great timbers, the convenience of backyard resources eliminated the difficulties of transporting heavy loads of stone or wood.

From the start, Pennsylvania barn builders used the balistratas, the fortress-like slits, for ventilation and circulation to dry the hay and grains. In later developments, builders made brick vents set into stone. Then came fixed wood louvers in frames. As time passed and the understanding of rising heat became clearer, ventilating cupolas appeared on roof ridges. Once glass and glazed-wood frames were developed, opening windows replaced the louvers to help light the barn interior as well as ventilate the heat.

Similar to English barns, the first steep-pitched German roofs were covered with the lightest materials available. These roofs were built with principal rafter construction techniques that used wide-set, heavy supports. They were covered with either straw thatch or, later on, long, hand-split shingles of white cedar, pine, or oak. When the slate beds in eastern Pennsylvania were discovered and "mined," slate tile roofing—on lower (or flatter) roof slopes—became common.

To protect the siding, early colonists smeared what was said to be a mix of iron-oxide and cows' milk onto their buildings. In Pennsylvania, once the prevailing deep red color had covered the wood-sided forebay, builders or owners trimmed the doorways, ventilators, and windows in lime whitewash or later, white lead paint.

When livestock populations increased on the farm, the amount of hay needed to feed the animals grew proportionately. Farmers stuffed barns with heavier and higher loads of feed. Forebays typically carried the granaries, and the rest of the space was used for general storage. Trapdoors in the floor and doors in the front wall opened to throw feed down to the livestock in the yard below. An exceptional harvest or several years of them displaced the tool storage and farmers piled hay high against the front walls as well. This strained the eighteenth- and nineteenth-century forebay engineering technology. At first, farmers and builders fabricated masonry columns to support the ends. Eventually, builders created sidewalls on the ground level, the stable level. Around 1800, stone masons simply began to build full gable walls down to the ground, without the notch below the forebay. Visually, this filled in the area under the ends of the cantilevered section. These walls supported the forebay at the point where the weight of hay and of the corner of the roof had previously hung out in the air. Frequently wood posts or masonry pillars were inserted beneath the bent posts along the forebay to provide further support.

But it was not only considerations of heavier hay loads that dictated these sidewalls or stone columns that began to appear beneath the forebay. The forests were being used up. Throughout the eighteenth century, summer beams could be cut to dimensions of 12x18 inches, in lengths of 50 or 60 feet. It was not uncommon to find cantilever beams running the entire width of a barn and stretching out into space 6, 8, or even 10 feet over the yard below. But these timbers were harvested out in the 1800s. Builders began to splice plates together to make up the length necessary to anchor the long forebay wall. Posts or columns were required to support the beams. The depletion of building materials forced architectural evolution.

Unfortunately this lovely construction has been taken down. As population growth continued, especially on the east end of Long Island, New York, the owners sold the farm and the barn was destroyed to make way for new housing.

CHAPTER 3

TECHNOLOGY SHAPES THE BARN

By the end of the eighteenth century emerging technologies promised to change the complexion of agricultural life. In 1784, Andrew Meikle displayed his first wheat and rye grain-threshing machine. In 1786, Ezekiel Reed showed off a machine he invented that cut narrow, wedge-shaped nails from sheet iron, which would revolutionize construction not only of barns but of all other buildings.

Round dairy barn, Hancock Shaker Village, Hancock, Massachusetts
It may have taken inspiration from the round threshing barn George Washington built at Mount Vernon, Virginia, but the Shakers constructed their 85-foot-diameter structure for milking purposes. The shed and silo came years later when the herd grew and the Shakers learned this was the only way to add on to a round barn.

Workers milked as many as 50 cows around the 46-foot-diameter central haymow, ending their task back where they started. The barn stretches 53 feet to the top of its central ventilation shaft. Built in 1826, it was a bank-barn design, building the barn on a hillside so hay wagons could drive in above the cattle, allowing farmers to use gravity to get feed to the stock.

Independence, in conjunction with technology, changed agriculture and life in America. One man directly affected by this was President George Washington, who by 1789 was more anxious to return home to Mount Vernon than to run the new nation. He had begun in the 1780s an ongoing written correspondence with Arthur Young in Great Britain. Young was known as a progressive farmer and thinker, one who came up with the new ideas that people such as Washington embraced.

Even as Washington commanded his army, his mind never strayed far from his farm. He had sought Young's ideas and thoughts on what might be the best plans for an English threshing barn at that time. Young responded quickly, suggesting a wood-sided, timber-frame structure built on a plan that was large enough to accommodate three men threshing in the center aisle at the same time.

Washington, aware of the difference of scale of operations between Young's England and his own Virginia, made two changes to the plans. When he had the new barn built on his Union Farm, he specified brick instead of wood siding; there was plenty of clay on his land. In addition, Washington's version allowed enough floor space for 30 men to thresh indoors without flailing one another. In this way, his slaves could work no matter what the weather outside the barn.

The plan worked well; the barn was completed in 1789, and for the next few years, its capacity was never exceeded. But Washington once again had been called to government service, this time as first president of the United States. He spent more and more time in New York and Philadelphia, the latter of which became the nation's capital in 1790. On one of his trips home in late 1792, he went to visit the large barn and found a full-fledged grain threshing operation going on—out in the yard in front of the barn. However, the men were not flailing the grain, they were using shod horses to separate the grain from its stalks. The men paraded the animals around in teams, letting the horses' weight do the job and the men followed, raking and scooping up the loose grains. It was not exactly a new innovation, but it certainly was not what Washington wanted, because too much grain was lost into the hard soil, and too much of what was recovered needed to be cleaned.

Almost immediately, Washington sketched the rudiments of a new idea. Horse and oxen "treading" to thresh the grain was a well-known idea and he had read of farms where planks were laid surrounding a barn. As the animals trod

Cross-gabled barn, Redman farm, McComb, Illinois
As innovative as the Shaker's round barn, but older, this square barn was derived from a Massachusetts meeting house plan that dated to 1702. Two competing builders during the summer of 1895 and 1896 populated a portion of central Illinois with these interesting barns. This building measures 40x40 but stands 52 feet tall.

The idea behind a square barn with crossed gables was to provide the maximum usable space with the fewest interior support beams. Doors on the center of each of the four walls opened to provide access for wagons, farm draft animals, and live stock. Building crews worked for $1 a day and finished a barn like this one each week.

laps around the barn, the threshing work got done. But of course, this was only a fair weather operation.

He needed a new barn. It was a short step from the rectangular English threshing barn with a treading ring in the barnyard to his own circular threshing barn with the animals working inside.

Washington designed a 52-foot diameter, 16-sided barn with a conical roof, to be built up against a rise. Washington's plan called for his threshing horses or oxen to enter from the south on the threshing floor level. They could tread around two or three abreast while Washington's slaves threw fresh grain beneath their hooves and shoveled away the wheat straw and animal waste behind them. He designed the threshing floor with gaps 1.5 inches wide running around the circle through which the threshed grains would fall, landing on a solid wood floor below. In the center of the upper level was unthreshed grain storage, while in the center of the lower level was a collection of grain bins.

The structure was built of oak, pine, and cypress. Its roof, with a fairly standard 43-degree pitch, was covered in cypress shingles. The lower level was built of brick fired on the farm (as the big English barn had been), and Washington incorporated barred windows not only to allow ventilation for drying but also to keep out thieves.

In the end, the barn would have had problems similar to horse treading in the yard. Animal waste could not always be caught by a quick shovel. When it came time for Washington to build a new threshing barn, Washington's men used a machine and not horses' hooves for threshing his grain.

Five hundred miles to the north, a group of recent English immigrants struggled to solve their own problems. In eastern New York, a United Society of Shaking Quakers was establishing its Church of Hancock in western Massachusetts. Persecuted by the English church, the 39-year-old founder, Mother Ann Lee and eight others came to New York in 1774.

Gambrel-roof dairy barn, near Fargo, North Dakota
By the time farmers reached the upper Midwest, barn building techniques were considerably modified over the English- and New England-style barns. Builders kept the New England-style gable-end entry but milled lumber rather than hand-hewn timber was the building material. The gambrel, or bent-gable-style, roof offered farmers greater interior capacity in the haymows.

Although Mother Ann and the Society were headquartered in New Lebanon, New York, Mother Ann traveled frequently and in 1783 she and church elders spent a month preaching and converting new believers around Hancock, in western Massachusetts. By the time Mother Ann died in 1784, her influence had spread throughout New England. Within a dozen years, believers established communities on 11 sites in five states. The Church of Hancock was founded in 1791.

Throughout the next 35 years, new members joined the Society and the population grew. Living quarters, segregating women from the men, were expanded, and new barns, sheds, meeting houses, and other buildings were constructed to meet the needs of a community of nearly 250 inhabitants.

In 1825, a fire destroyed the largest cow barn, located near the center of the Church Family settlement. When Elder William Deming and Elder Daniel Goodrich—in whose home Mother Ann had held the first worship service in Hancock—began to think about replacing the structure, they devised a round, banked barn with a low conical roof topped by a round cupola.

The purpose of their barn was not for threshing grain but for storing feed for their large herd of dairy and beef cattle. Like Washington, the Shakers utilized the tall center area of their barns for storage. They filled this cavity by driving a wagon up into the barn and unloading hay or grain down into the center. Both barns used gravity to good advantage, Washington's to deliver the trod-out grain to storage bins below, the Shakers' to deliver hay to cattle feeding and being milked below. The 85-foot, 10-inch outside diameter of the Massachusetts barn dwarfed Washington's 52-foot scale, but the Shakers needed space to milk as many as 50 cows at a

English-style tobacco barn, Mt. Orab, Ohio
By the late nineteenth century, tobacco barns were constructed with drying doors along their long sides. This 40x73-foot structure features 16-inch-wide panels nearly 16 feet tall. These remain open day and night to allowplenty of circulation around the fresh leaves.

time. The central hay location meant that one individual could feed the entire milking herd with few wasted steps. Stanchions and head guards separated and secured the cows, and milking began and ended in the same place around the circle every day.

They framed the large barn mostly with chestnut and used either pine, chestnut, or other local woods for the hay wagon level flooring and the roof. The limestone, fieldstone, and low grade marble used for the walls was quarried locally. Construction took nearly a year.

The Shakers devised a number of interesting safety features in the barn. Even with stone walls that ranged in thickness from 3 feet at the base to 2 feet at the eaves, fire was a great risk. Draft horses that hauled in the heavily loaded hay wagons were fitted with forged-steel horseshoes. Thirty chestnut 8x12-inch floor beams, each 16 feet, 3 inches long, supported the haymow wagon floor. On top of the 8x12s,

5x8 "sleepers" were pegged in, equally spaced from the outside stone wall to the haymow low wall. Onto these, the carpenters nailed pine subfloor planks. However, because of the risk of a horseshoe striking a nail head and causing a spark, Deming and Goodrich ordered a second pine plank floor laid on top of the subfloor. It was not secured with nails. Basically, it floated. Its nearly 16-foot width allowed for horses and wagons to circle around the open haymow. The full circle, like Washington's structure, eliminated the need to back horses and wagons out of the barn.

Vertical beams that extended up to the roof peak, each 6x8-inch 53-foot-tall, formed a central, octagonal-shaped open column. This allowed ventilation to the middle of the hay pile. At the bottom, the entire mound of hay sat on another false floor, this one built nearly a foot above the pounded dirt. This also allowed air to circulate to the bottom of the hay pile. Below the cattle level, around the perimeter of the barn, was a manure sink; the milkers and barn attendants shoveled the animal waste down through trapdoors spaced around the outside of the milking parlor. In the common practice of the day, this was allowed to build up through the winter to insulate the ground from frosts. In the spring the accumulated manure was hauled out and spread over the fields as fertilizer.

The Shakers completed the barn in 1826 and it performed as intended for almost 40 years. Then, on December 1, 1864, a fire caused by a carelessly handled lantern destroyed the conical roof, its structural support members, and much of the timber framework within the barn.

There was no question but to rebuild. Within a year, the barn was cleaned out, reframed, and the roof was rebuilt. Its new roof was nearly flat, but it was crowned by a 15-foot-tall cupola in the center, similar to what had been at the point of the cone before this. A decade later, the roof was modified once more. A 14-sided 51-foot, 10-inch diameter structure was built. This added nearly 9 feet to the height of the barn and was fitted with double-hung windows to allow not only for additional ventilation but also to provide greater daytime illumination. The 15-foot-tall cupola was replaced on the roof of the clerestory structure at its center.

Because it required members to remain celibate, virtually no one was born into the Shaker faith, and in the first half of the twentieth century it acquired few converts. The Shaker population drastically declined. In 1959, with only three elderly sisters surviving at Hancock, the Central Ministry located in Canterbury, New Hampshire, decided to close the Massachusetts village. On October 15, 1960, the remaining 900 acres and 17 buildings still standing were sold, and restoration of the village that had long been neglected began soon after.

Once the active dairy farming ceased and no new manure insulated the shallow foundation, frost heaved and unsettled the round stone building. Walls cracked. In February 1968, workers began a near-complete renovation of the round barn. All of the existing stonework was dismantled, leaving only the concentric roofs supported by timber-frame skeletons. Some of the stone was exchanged for new material quarried expressly for the restoration. Window and door lintels were replaced.

While the Shaker faith declined in popularity, the popularity of round barns increased. By the mid-1920s there were more round barns than there were Shakers.

The scale of farming requires larger barns but practices remain unchanged. Recently harvested tobacco leaves fill the "rooms" of this drying barn. A room is about 4x12 feet, designed to fit the complicated system of stalks and staves. A barn this size may contain as much as 36,000 pounds of leaves hanging from 12,000 or more of the 4-foot staves.

CHAPTER 4

FADS & FALSE STARTS

When the first settlers reached the Midwest, they found plains and grasslands extending on to the next horizon. This land was meant for wheat and corn. The foodstuffs required to feed the growing urban populations in the East meshed perfectly with the Midwest's ability to produce huge crops. Cheap freight was the icing on the cake. The economical movement of goods from western parts of the country had a profound effect on New England farmers.

Connected New England-style barn, Wheeler farm, Hardwick, Massachusetts
This banked barn is connected to the farmhouse through common walls to a workshop, a large kitchen, and then the main house. This large farm also had a dairy operation so the barn attached to the house sheltered only their horses and carriages.

With the large haymow above the stables, it was an easy matter to shovel down the horse feed through openings in the ceiling for the three carriage horses here. Carriage storage, a tack room, and a small office filled the ground floor. The barn has a full basement, now used as a boarding kennel.

Farming conditions in New England were always challenging. The land was rocky and rolling. The earth was littered with rocks and the topsoil was shallow and not very fertile. Finally, no matter what the crop was, the growing season was short and unpredictable. Some years provided as few as 100 frost-free days to Maine farmers; 160 was a good, generous season.

The farmers who survived were neither stupid nor backward. They read farm journals, they experimented with new crops, new home industries, new techniques, and new building styles. They made dramatic changes when they thought improvements and benefits would result.

In New England around the beginning of the nineteenth century, the largest, most progressive farmers made a big change in the design of their barns. The English barn, with its main doorway in the center of the sidewall, gave way to the New England barn in which the main doorway was placed on the gable end.

The English barn was part of the English tradition that dictated separate structures for different tasks. The New England barn allowed a variety of operations to be incorporated under one roof. Its popularity spread throughout the next 30 years to even the smallest farms.

One curious development influenced this change from the English to the New England style for a short while. Each of these barns was still basically a three-bay-by-three-aisle

design. The center aisle in the English barns had been the threshing floor. But by the early 1830s, threshing machines began to replace hand threshing and the center floor became equipment storage. In addition, because machine threshing—and horse-drawn farming—was more efficient and more productive with greater yield, farmers discovered the need for more room in the haymow and granary.

Between the 1830s and the 1850s, another development spread widely throughout New England. Barns built from scratch were constructed on top of a cellar, and those already existing had one dug out from underneath. This provided storage areas both for the livestock manure—no longer hauled out of the barn but simply shoveled through trapdoors into the cellar below—as well as for some of the crops meant for consumption or shipping at a later date.

All of these improvements in barn design and construction set the stage for the next, most significant step in the evolution of the New England barn: its connection to the farmer's house.

From the earliest days of farmhouses in New England, summer kitchens were joined to the rear of the house in a kind of L-shaped addition, often called the "little house." This kept the heat of cooking out of the rest of the house in the summer months. Beginning in the late 1700s, a further addition to the structure that was strung off the back of the kitchen housed the farmer's workshop. The candle making,

Connected New England barn, Skolfield farm, Harpswell Neck, Maine
The Skolfields of Maine were eminent whaling ship builders but as each builder retired and each captain came home, they turned to farming. They built and added on to a large connected four-home, two-barn complex that, when completed, stretched nearly 300 feet.

The large barn, built in 1897, is just shy of 40x85 feet and was capable of a large dairy operation. The smaller barn at the other end of the long complex was just 32x36, and was constructed in 1834. Called Merrucoonegan Farm, the name means "carrying place across the neck" between two bays.

leather tanning, cabinet making, or other home industry was done in here as well. While the English farm would have separated each function into a distant building, writers in farming magazines in the mid-1800s began to stress saving steps and centralizing all the farm's activities closer to the main house. And so the "back house" —the shops—joined the little house.

Magazine writers stressed the efficiency available to farmers and families from connecting barn to carriage house to workshop to kitchen to main house. The barns that farmers attached to their string of other structures were often simply moved from somewhere else in the farmyard to join the house. Or else a barn was torn down and its pieces used to construct a new barn connected to the carriage house or work shed. (This was easier, of course, because barns prior to 1850 simply rested on—but were not usually attached to— excavated cellars or rudimentary foundations of stone.)

Farmers in New England continued to build barns connected to their homes all the way into the early 1900s. But the style never moved west too far beyond Massachusetts. In fact,

the preponderance of these wonderful buildings were built and are still found in Maine, southern New Hampshire, southeastern Vermont, and eastern and central Massachusetts.

That this style was never adopted in Minnesota or in the Dakotas and Montana where winters are far more severe explains in itself why the connected barn was not a weatherwise development. These connected barns came to exist as a result of —and to improve the results of—home industry.

It was, in effect, a kind of fad. It provided one more futile attempt to make a challenging farming condition into something more successful than it was. Agriculture alone could no longer provide an income that would support New England farmers. In the face of an economically threatening challenge from the open prairies of the Midwest, almost no industry or idea seemed too radical to open-minded farmers bent on survival.

Connected farm buildings were not the only fad that farmers adopted in the interest of efficiency and increased productivity. Franklin Hiram King picked up and vigorously promoted an innovation adopted by George Washington and the Hancock Village Shakers. King, a professor of agricultural physics at the University of Wisconsin-Madison, was asked to design an inexpensive dairy barn that would accommodate eight cows and ten horses and that would permit extra space for driving behind the cattle for cleaning, and in front of them for feeding green fodder. A silo, granary, and storage space for dry fodder was to be covered by the same roof.

Without acknowledging the origins of his design, Franklin King devised something very similar to the Hancock Shaker barn, which he enlarged slightly. He proposed that his brother, C.E. King, who had posed the challenge to Franklin, build this new circular barn out of wood on a stone foundation. King even reproduced the George Washington-Hancock Village conical roof with its attached center cupola. In his plan for his brother, Franklin replaced the center haymow of the Shaker barn with a round silo, which was his own innovation; before King, silos were square and separated from the barn. This internal silo was 34 feet tall with a 28-foot outside diameter.

The King circular barn, completed in 1891, was 92 feet in diameter and it stood 28 feet from the ground to the eaves. The bottom floor was configured in three concentric circles. Cows faced out from the innermost ring to a middle aisle from which they were fed. Cows also occupied the outer ring, facing back into the middle one. The animals stood on a raised wood floor for milking; to their rear was a 6-foot-wide wagon path for manure cleanup. On the second level, above the cows and the feed aisle, was a hay floor extending out 18 feet from the edge of the silo. This held the loose hay, which could be forked down to the livestock below through a series of trapdoors. Around the outside wall of the second floor, above the outer milking ring and its wagon path, was the hay wagon floor. Here, just as in the Hancock barn, horse-drawn wagons entered by a ramp and unloaded while moving around the circle. The horses then walked out without having to back up.

The barn foundation was also a series of concentric circles. The innermost one supported the silo, while the outside ring carried the walls.

King had been concerned for some time with barn ventilation. His design allowed the heat of drying hay and silage to escape through the cupola. As the heat rose, it drew in fresh, cool air from holes drilled through from the outside at the sills. King's design offered one more benefit. Ensilage stored inside the center silo was insulated from outside freezing temperatures by the large air space surrounding it and by the considerable body heat generated by the livestock wintering inside the barn.

Unfortunately for the brothers King, Franklin's roof did not hold up well on C.E.'s barn. In an attempt to provide a clear span through the haymow, King put no supports under his diagonal roof rafters forming the cone. Over time, the weight of the cupola coupled with the strain regularly put on the roof rafters by the heavily loaded hay fork began to put the entire roof in jeopardy of collapsing. Designers who followed King's invention quickly adopted supported gambrel roofs and later trussed gambrels and arches.

Estimates suggest that as many as 215 round or polygonal barns were constructed in Wisconsin. Another 170 were

Octagon barn, Sheildt farm, Edgerton, Wisconsin
Originally built for dairy farming around 1909, this eight-sided barn was strongly influenced by writings from University of Wisconsin-Madison researcher Frank King. This is one in an area of barns built by noted builder Aga Shivers.

built in Minnesota and 160 in Iowa. King's design appeared not only in the extension service report, but it was also reproduced in all six editions of a very popular agricultural science textbook he authored. Eventually, King's cause was taken up by others. A professional colleague at the University of Illinois at Champaign-Urbana, Wilbur J. Frazer, published an article called "Economy of the Round Dairy Barn." It was Frazer's enthusiasm that spread the popularity of round barns not only throughout Illinois but on to Indiana as well. Between 250 and 300 were constructed in Indiana, and that state claims that it is the round barn capital of America.

Round barns offered farmers different farming techniques from traditional rectangular or even octagonal barns. The incorporation of a silo within the barn mandated that interior arrangements be reconfigured. Straight rows would be interrupted by the silo; stalls, feeding, and cleaning alleys all curved around it. The top of the silo often became the center support for the barn roof, alleviating the need for all other interior posts and opening up all but the center of the barn to free span.

The next development to affect Franklin King's round silo also benefited the round barn. At Iowa State University, Professor J. B. Davidson and Iowa Experiment Station researcher Matt King worked with a local tile manufacturer to produce the first clay tiles for round silos in 1908. From that success, they developed hollow curved tiles, which they then promoted for barn construction as a fire-safe and less expensive alternative to wood.

Owners saw other alternatives for their farms because of the round barn. Before the turn of the twentieth century, farmers had begun to specialize. Barns strictly intended for dairy operations started to appear. Other barns were being designed to house specific stock such as beef cattle, sheep, or hogs. Some structures were being constructed as show barns for the display and sales of livestock brought in only for that purpose.

Round barn plans could be ordered by mail. A Chicago architect William Radford, who had produced barn plans beginning in the 1890s, sold round barn plans for $20 and blueprints for an octagonal barn for $15 as early as 1909. William Louden, the Fairfield, Iowa, barn equipment manufacturer, produced and sold round barn blueprints for $5 in 1915. Matt King, the agricultural engineer who had helped develop the curved hollow tiles, began to provide his own plans through the Permanent Building Society of Des Moines. Davenport, Iowa, prefabricated house manufacturer Gordon-Van

Tine Company, offered pre-cut, ready-to-assemble round barn kits in their 1917 catalog. Chicago mail-order houses Montgomery Ward and Sears Roebuck each offered kits. Sears' customers could even finance the barn and arrange for its assembly by Sears' carpenters through the catalog.

In southeastern Wisconsin, Alga Shivers, a carpenter-builder, earned quite a reputation building round barns. Shivers was one of a group of blacks who settled into Cheyenne Valley near Ontario, Wisconsin, following the Civil War. He constructed nearly a dozen barns throughout the small area.

Already known as a barn builder, Shivers began to receive orders for round barns in the late 1890s from farmers inspired by King's writings. Shivers and his small crew harvested wood from the farmer's own forest and left the wood to cure. A year or so later, he and two or three assistants would arrive in their wagons and begin construction. The work usually took Shivers and his crew about three months to complete.

The popularity of the style failed abruptly in the late 1920s. Technology was partly to blame. Loose hay was baled more often than not by then, and putting up bales into a round mow was difficult. Barn cleaners and hay trolleys were widely marketed by companies such as Louden, Janesway, and others. Their systems didn't work in structures built by independents such as Shivers or Benton Steele because no two independent round barns had the same diameter so standard curves could not be adapted to individual circular gutters and walls. A similar problem arose with the adoption of milking machines. The pipes at first were not easily bent into gradual arcs.

An element of greed played a role as well. Horace Duncan, a Midwestern architect, succeeded in obtaining a patent for a round barn design in the early 1920s. He demanded a royalty and took to suing for patent infringement anyone who copied the idea of the round barn, let alone his own version of it. Word spread quickly.

The real causes of the death of the round barns, however, were deeper. The success and growth of some farms was one influence. While builders like Alga Shivers always counseled their customers to build a bigger barn than they needed at that moment, many did not, and built instead only what they could afford. Later, when they wanted or needed to expand their herd, the round barn couldn't grow longer or wider. It couldn't grow up or out. As George Washington discovered,

16-sided mule barn, Graham farm, Denver, North Carolina
Alexander Graham, the progressive agricultural commissioner of North Carolina, constructed this center-aisle 16-sided barn to house his mules around 1905. This 59-foot-"diameter" structure was based on octagonal designs by Lorenzo Coffin and Elliott Stewart, just as Franklin King and others began promoting round dairy barns.

it could only be supplemented—or replaced—with another round, or more likely, rectangular barn.

However, the lack of success of farms was a greater cause. The Great Depression halted almost all farm construction, and by the time farmers could afford to build again (after World War II), round barns—and traditional barns gener-

ally—had ceased to be practical. The round barn worked with horse farming, but the advent of tractor farming doomed the concept. Even the largest round barn seldom had enough alley space to allow entry of a tractor with a front-end loader, which became necessary for the efficient removal of manure by the middle of the twentieth century.

CHAPTER 5

WESTERN BARNS

From the 1840s through the 1890s, Eastern and Midwestern farmers moved to the West and became ranchers. Without irrigation, there was grass enough to feed cows but scarcely enough per acre to maintain a viable dairy operation the likes of which were beginning back East. This was land to let the stock range free, loosely tended.

These low-eave, long-roofed structures are sometimes called Mormon cattle barns. This 53x59-foot structure houses an office, tack room, three 8x10-foot box stalls, and two long foaling pens around the central 20x40-foot open hay storage. The hay hood, at the peak of the roof, allowed a rail-suspended hayfork to lift the feed from wagons outside the barn and sling it inside on to the top of a pile too high for a fork to throw.

Along with box stalls, this barn provides a 20x40-foot central hay and feed storage and two large foaling pens along the rear and one side. Ranchers often stabled their horses and kept winter feed dry inside the barn, riding out with wagons to feed snowbound cattle.

These animals required larger and larger ranches but because this "crop" generally walked to market on its own four feet, few of these ranches had need for barns, until specific uses dictated otherwise. While dairy farms in the East and Midwest wintered their herds inside barns, this was impossible in the West. Instead, ranchers risked everything each winter, relying on their steers to forage for grass beneath the lighter snows of lower elevations. However, this risk was self-perpetuating: even small herds needed a lot of range. But small herds were subsistence ranching; it was large herds that made money, and they required vast lands. Any profit from the stock sale would be squandered in the expense of building a barn large enough to house them all and their winter's feed. Instead, smaller structures held feed that was ridden out daily to widespread herds.

Western barns were rare and specialized. In California, Oregon, Washington, and Idaho, they were home to the large horse herds needed to harvest wheat. Elsewhere—Montana, Wyoming, and Colorado, for example—they stored feed to supplement winter grazing. Many of the structures were built out of local indigenous materials. Most were low to the ground, cowering beneath winter jet streams that blasted hard winds down from the Arctic Circle. Those winds slapped too hard against the tall, traditional Yankee barns of New England, and builders attempting to bring Eastern and Midwestern traditions to the windswept West found their barns collapsed under January blizzards.

John William "Peter" French built some of the more specialized barns in the West. French worked for Hugh James Glenn, operating Glenn's vast ranching operations.

Hugh Glenn was born in Virginia in 1824. He was a doctor during the Mexican War, but when miners in California discovered gold at Sutter's Mill east of Sacramento, Glenn bought some livestock in Missouri and drove them all the way to gold country. Hungry for beef, the market bought whatever was available and paid—in gold—whatever the seller asked.

Glenn made a dozen trips back to Missouri. He returned with cattle, horses, and sheep, each time taking from hungry miners their hard-found gold. By 1867, Glenn had acquired a 7,000-acre land grant in northern Colusa County, north of Sacramento, eventually growing his ranch to 70,000 acres.

Glenn hired 21-year-old "Peter" French in 1870. In 1872, Glenn sent French north with a select herd of 1,200 shorthorn cows, a few bulls, about 20 saddle horses, half a dozen

Mormon cattle barn, Lewallen ranch, Lake View, Oregon
In the far West, barn builders modified English and Dutch floor plans to fit available materials and prevalent weather conditions. Low eaves and limited end gable exposure to high winds characterize most Western barns. This roof design is called gable-on-hip-roof.

Horse barn, Werner/Hamel farm, Davis, California

This barn, its southern face re-sided with corrugated steel, was built first in Connecticut in 1860, then disassembled and shipped by boat to San Francisco for reassembly in Davis, about 100 miles east. Owner Frederick Werner had the 40x101 originally sided with redwood. He later added a 14-foot stable shed on the east side.

Henry Hamel bought the 1,200-acre farm from Werner in 1876 and raised Clydesdale and Percheron draught horses to sell to San Francisco trolley car and waterfront shipping companies. The barn, framed of eastern hemlock and pine, contains 26 horse stalls, an office, tack room, and bunkroom.

Horse breaking barn, P Ranch, near Frenchglen, Oregon
Cattle rancher Peter French devised and built three of these round barns for his ranch hands to break horses. The 30-foot-tall center drops to 8-foot walls at its outer edges, the better to resist strong north winds while providing maximum interior space.

The structure spreads 96 feet across, with a 60-foot diameter breaking corral surrounded by 2-foot-thick stone walls and a 14-foot-wide outer exercise track. French and his crews hauled juniper trees for framing and rafters and cedar for shingles—as well as about 250 tons of lava rock—more than 50 miles to build the barns. They broke about 200 wild horses a year in this barn.

Horse barn, Valley Farm, Harrington, Washington
In 1888, the California Land & Stock Co. housed 300 horses in this 33x243-foot barn. California Land acquired 28 sections of land from the Northern Pacific on speculation after learning the railroad planned its route through Harrington. The horses (and mules by the 1920s) dragged plows and rippers, breaking ground for farming.

vaqueros, and a Chinese cook. French encountered a disillusioned gold miner named Porter working the Donner and Blitzen Valley in southeast Oregon. Porter owned a dozen cows and he readily sold them and his branding iron, the "P," to French. This conferred to French the right to every other steer with a P on its hip. More important, it conveyed the grazing rights in the valley where P cattle had fed.

The valley Porter occupied had enjoyed unusual rain during the previous 15 years. Porter had the entire valley to himself, grazing in the shadow of the 50-mile-long, 9,354-foot-high Steens Mountain. When French and his crew and the 1,212 head of cattle walked down into the valley, they met grass up to their saddle stirrups. For French it was love at first sight. He decided to own it as far as he could see.

When neighboring rancher Bill Barton retired, French bought his ranch, which included a vast gentle hilltop that was

dry year 'round even in wet years. On that rise, French built the first of his new barns, round ones, meant for horse breaking.

French reasoned that his men had little to do during the deep winter months. Yet horse breaking was just not practical in the snow, so he conceived a large round barn supported in the center by a single, 35-foot-tall, 1-foot-diameter juniper tree. A ring of 13 similar junipers circled the center post 14 feet out, and another 14 feet beyond that a 24-inch thick volcanic stone wall marked the edge of the circular breaking corral. French's men hauled 170 cubic yards of the rock—about 250 tons—8 miles by wagon from the river. Fourteen windows—simple woodframed holes left in the stone walls actually—allowed light into the corral. Outside the stone wall was another 14-foot-wide dirt track surrounded by the 8-foot-tall wood-plank outer wall that held up the roof rafters. Lumber for the two gates, the rafters,

Mennonite connected dairy and horse barn, Hamm farm, Altoona, Manitoba

Sunrise reflects in the windows of the house and connected barn, built together around 1876. The structure differs from New England connected barns because in these structures there is direct access from the 24x38-foot house into the 33x83-foot barn through a "mud room" doorway, an advantage in January when temperatures drop to -40 degrees Fahrenheit.

and siding was milled in Burns, 55 miles north. The entire barn was 96 feet in diameter.

The barn worked so well that French built two more. The French-Glenn operation reached a point where it raised about 300 head of horses and mule colts each year. French's men broke even more wild horses—some stories say as many as 1,000 each year—that the men captured running free. Beyond the 200 to 300 that the P needed to operate, French sold the rest.

Exact dates of the round barn construction are uncertain. Educated guesses suppose that they were built before 1880. Cattle ranching, especially in the West, had limited uses for barns. Herds were much too large to stable through the winters. With the exception of structures already existing on the ranches Peter French bought, there were few barns. It appears he and his men built only one rectangular barn in addition to the three round ones.

No one knows where Peter French got the idea to enclose a horse-breaking corral within a riding track, all under one roof. He was an extremely intelligent man, and he was a reader. It's likely that the popular journals that publicized Orson Fowler, Elliott Stewart, Franklin King, and Wilbur Frazer also reached the West and found their way into Peter French's saddle bags and on up to the P ranch.

In February 1883, Peter French married Hugh Glenn's daughter Ella. Just 16 days after the wedding, 58-year old Hugh Glenn was shot in the head by his former bookkeeper. His estate was valued at $1.23 million, including 30,000 head of cattle on the 70,000-acre ranch that French had built for him in Oregon.

The day after Christmas 1898, French helped his men to move a herd, working in place of one of his sick foremen. The group watched as neighboring rancher Ed Oliver rode out of a hollow at full gallop, charging them. Within moments, he

The Mennonite community issued strict guidelines for farm organization, each homestead being 1/4 section, 160 acres, but oriented for mutual protection. All the parcels were long narrow pieces and the house and barn fit longitudinally, with the house nearest the road. Horses and cows, needing daily attention, lived in the attached barn, while pigs and chickens were housed in separate structures.

Livestock barn, New Dungeness Lightstation, New Dungeness, Washington
The United States Lighthouse Establishment put Cape Cod-style cottages and New England barns in the West in 1857, regardless of what other barn and home builders were doing. Living miles from the nearest towns, the keepers had to raise their own food in sometimes incredibly difficult conditions. Government architect Ammi Young designed the tower, cottages, and the barn that, for its first century, housed a cow and horse.

shot French in the face with a pistol. Peter French died immediately. A jury trial found Oliver not guilty.

The cowboy violence of the West that ended the lives of cattleman Hugh Glenn and barn innovator Peter French was a far cry from the experiences of the peaceable and equally innovative Mennonites in North America.

By the time the Mennonites arrived in Manitoba in the 1870s, they'd been pushed around Western and Eastern Europe for early 300 years. Their story began in the Netherlands and Switzerland during the Reformation, where the religious sect was founded by followers of a Dutch priest called Menno Simmons. They wanted a clear separation between church and state. The emerging governments in the sixteenth century, however, seemed to them to exist solely to make war. The Mennonites refused to swear loyalty or to fight, and they could not support the state-approved churches. To the governments, then, the Mennonites were a new enemy.

Their strong beliefs resulted in their expulsion from many cities throughout Western Europe during the late

1500s. They were welcomed in Poland where the royalty recognized the value of a peaceful nature and an industrious work ethic.

Their refusal to bear arms, to serve a state, or to declare loyalty to any government again made them refugees in 1772 when Prussia took over the lands that the Mennonites had peaceably inhabited for nearly 200 years. Between 1789 and 1830, most of the nearly 3,700 Mennonite families living in Poland went on to southern Russia, invited by Catherine the Great.

For the purpose of equality, the Mennonite farmers gave all their fields to the village. All the land was divided equally among the families. Each was given a long, narrow plot that extended back from the river. Houses were built—or moved—to be near the river or around a common grazing pasture, and cultivation took place in long rows out the rear. The connected house-barns ended up side-by-side, with an equal distance between them, offering protection against invading Tartars.

Some 85 Mennonite communities flourished in Russia. But again, politics interfered. In the 1870s, neighboring German nations flexed their muscle. Russia reacted by seeking to make all its inhabitants "Russian." Their language became a mandatory study in schools and only Russian was accepted for official correspondence. A Universal Military Service Act in 1874 reminded many Mennonites of Prussian requirements 100 years before. They resolved to move once again. Throughout the next 10 years, some 18,000 Mennonites immigrated to North America. Eight thousand of them headed to Canada, to the new province of Manitoba. The rest scattered into Minnesota, South Dakota, Nebraska, and Kansas.

The first Mennonites into Canada negotiated reserves of land starting in Steinbach, southeast of Winnipeg. Families began to arrive in 1874. By 1875, they expanded into the Western Reserve of lands held for them. They named their new communities Altona, Neubergthal, and Chortitz and other names carried over from Ukraine. The village design established in southern Russia was also carried over to this new homeland. Farms were laid out long and narrow. Each house was set 60 meters from the next, each one set back 30 meters from the road. A portion of land was set aside for nonfarmers and another for community buildings such as stores, post offices, schools, and blacksmith shops. From the first arrivals in 1875 until the railroad reached the area in 1882, most of the buildings were temporary log structures, quickly assembled, and covered with mud or sod. These were half submerged into the ground and consisted of two "rooms," the larger for the family, the smaller for the livestock. These roughly 15x35-foot structures were relatively warm throughout Manitoba's brutal winter due to the shared body heat of the inhabitants.

As in Russia, the Mennonites in Manitoba set their connected house-barn buildings perpendicular to the road and always facing either east or south. Their first permanent homes originally comprised only four rooms in front of the barns.

By the time this generation left Russia for North America, brick had been used for building for all their lives. Neighboring settlers had to show the newcomers how to build with logs. The post-and-fill technique was widely adopted. Carpenters squared the timbers by adze or saw for posts, sills, plates, and corner braces. They filled the hollow walls with round logs. They cut tongues into the ends that fit into vertical grooves

Not surrounded by vast fields of tillable soil, the lighthouse keepers at the end of the 7-mile-long sand spit worked hard to raise vegetables and keep a small farm. The Lighthouse Service called every 90 days to supplement staples but keepers were expected to raise their own food as well.

they had sliced into the posts. The builders applied a thick mud plaster inside and out to keep the logs in place and insulate the interior. The newer houses were much larger, often up to 20x30 feet before the barn was added.

In the Mennonite communities, farmers generally built their barns a few years after the houses. In the interim, they wintered their livestock in the original log house. When the barn was built, it usually stretched twice the length of the house, but it was still attached to it, often sharing the same roof ridge line. It was generally slightly wider than the residence. Timber-frame construction used principal rafters at first, but then later, they went to common rafters. A small room called a gang led into the barn. The gang was a kind of air-lock that usually also provided access to the house cellar.

Typically the barns behind the houses were for horses and cows, with cows closest to the house and horses farther back. These were the animals that needed the hired man's attention every day. Pigs and chickens were in a separate building on the other side of the yard.

CHAPTER 6

MAKING WAY FOR PROGRESS

What started in 1793 with Eli Whitney and his cotton gin continued—and accelerated—throughout the next century and a half. Change, progress, and development became a product in the United States as important as anything produced on a farm or in a factory. In 1797, Charles Newbold received a patent for his one-piece cast-iron plow. The first hay mowing machines appeared in England in 1802.

Sawmill, Sorghum press, feed mill, Nelson farm, Marine on St. Croix, Minnesota
This complex structure represents farm as industry. Albert Nelson built his original 34x61-foot barn of oak around 1885 from timber milled at his own sawmill in the barn. The barn also housed his dairy herd but he soon established a 28x18-foot sorghum press shed and later a feed mill with a 36-foot tower.

High-drive, banked barn, Mountain Valley Farm, Waitsfield, Vermont
Built in 1882, this 46x116-foot dairy barn represented Vermont barn builders' best adaptive senses. Steep hillsides surrounding small valleys meant farmers left the valley floors for crops and built their homes and barns above them. Barn builders devised the high-drive style that moved hay and feed wagons into the barn at the top, near the roof peak, nearly 45 feet above the valley floor, so farmers enjoyed the benefit of gravity when they unloaded wagons to livestock below.

The mechanical cultivator was introduced in 1820. Samuel Lane received a patent for what may have been the first combined harvester and thresher in 1828. The next year, 1829, Patrick Bell developed his grain-reaping machine.

In 1831, Cyrus Hall McCormick introduced his mechanical grain reaper. In 1834, a Chicago blacksmith, John Lanel cut steel strips from a saw blade and wrapped them around the wood moldboard of his plow. To his satisfaction, he found that it sliced more easily through the sticky Midwest soil. A year later, in 1835, Hiram and John Pitt developed their efficient, stationary grain-threshing machine. John Deere began to produce plows in Illinois in 1837. In France in 1860, Léonce-Eugène Grassin-Baledans received his patent for twisting strands of sheet metal into fence material—generally considered to be the birth of barbed wire.

During this century of progress, American barn builders began to take what could be learned from earlier builders and apply it to their emerging needs. In many cases, the new structures reflected improvements and even innovations on existing techniques and ideas.

The benefits of the Pennsylvania Dutch banked barns traveled up and down the East Coast. In Vermont, towering timber-framed structures jutted from the rolling hills. Starting in the late 1880s, New England-style barns—with entries on their gable ends—built against steep hillsides began to appear. The geography of the numerous long, narrow valleys provided little truly flat land and farmers wanted this for cultivation. But the hillsides, while impossibly steep for horse teams and implements or later tractors to negotiate, offered barn builders the benefit of entry at several levels. As the roads, too, stayed out of the flats, access from the road to the barn was to the highest level of the structure, producing the so-called "high-drive" built near the roof peak. This heavy driveway lined with waist-high walls ran the full length of the barn, splitting the top level. Farmers drove their horse-drawn wagons onto these floors. Then, standing atop the piled loose hay, their heads near the rafters, they took advantage of gravity and pitched their hay down either side to the haymows below.

At first, after the wagons were empty, farmers gently fought the horses and wagons backward out the same driveway, but by 1895 many barn builders incorporated a turnaround along the way through the barn. Others built huge turntables. When the wagon was emptied, the farmers backed the wagons into the alcove or onto the rotating platform, walked the horses across the front, and proceeded out facing forward.

High-drive, banked barn, Locust Grove farm, East St. Johnsbury, Vermont

This 40x100 1911 barn utilized the 12x20-foot covered ramp to give weather protection to wagons entering the barn to unload hay and grain. Many Vermont builders provided this kind of structure, each individualizing the barn as they improved on their own designs. Inspecting these barns, with owner's permission, can reveal fascinating differences. Some builders signed their work; others were content to take the pay and move on anonymously.

Most barn builders constructed bridge-like ramps to provide wagon access to the high drive. This reduced the amount of excavation needed to get a barn of sufficient height near enough to a road. These bridges were soon enclosed in sometimes elaborate structures to ensure horse and wagon access even in winter snows. The bridges often had roof peak lines that ran unbroken off the roof of the barn.

Most of these barns followed common practices of the time. The dairy milking parlor was above the ground. Farmers used gravity again to aid in barn cleaning; manure was shoveled through trapdoors to the ground below. This served both as convenient winter storage for the wastes as well as essential ground insulation for the barn's foundation against New England winter frosts.

Building the entire barn above the ground to allow for this cellar/manure pit was a development that surely aided smaller farm operators. These farmers performed their daily chores with a minimum of help. For these farms, the most efficient cleanup was to shovel the waste through a trapdoor.

In areas where flat land was less of a premium, or where more prosperous farmers found additional manpower to be no financial burden, builders were always willing to accommodate. Sometimes they constructed large, lavish barns that reflected new ideas from leading magazines of the day.

Albert T. "Ab" Fancher was born into a family established in purebred cattle, but he had ambitions beyond beef. He was one of the earliest to acquire petroleum drilling leases in Oklahoma. He founded Seneca Oil Company, and by the early days of the twentieth century Ab Fancher's wells were pumping nearly 10,000 barrels a month.

Eventually Ab sold his oil interests to Standard Oil and bought a ranch in New York. In 1913 Ab's workers began construction of an enormous cattle barn that would incorporate calving pens, horse stables, and a bull-breeding house.

Dairy barn, Fancher/Valent family farm, Salamanca, New York

Albert Fancher, a New York state senator, operated a showplace dairy farm in the shadow of the Allegheny State Park and had open houses on Sundays with all his cows rubbed down with banana oil to disguise the aroma of manure. The 1,000-acre farm now runs 300 head of which current owners milk 100 of them three times daily. The side milking parlor is 185 feet long.

Monitor horse barn, Meadowfarm, Orange, Virginia
By 1900, farm journals and design books had taken the place of itinerant builders moving ideas across country. Architects published plans and retailers such as Sears Roebuck even sold houses and barns by catalog. Popular styles, and those not so common such as this monitor roof design, were available in balloon frame construction, delivered by rail and put up on site.

When Fancher died on March 30, 1930, the farm was taken over by Fancher's nephew, Tom Mills. Mills' expertise, however, was in gas and oil, like that of his uncle. With so much of his time obligated to business in Oklahoma, Mills sold the dairy cows. He planned to close down the property altogether when another cattle broker, Jim Valent, appeared. Mills sold him the stock and the ranch in late 1939.

The Fancher/Valent barn reflected contemporary magazine thinking that suggested treating dairy and beef cattle business as something similar to a factory operation.

This Sears barn model, the Springvale Horse barn, measured 38x71. Sears used yellow pine for framing, flooring, and sheathing and cypress for siding and doors. Sears' monitor left the extended cupola sparsely sided for maximum ventilation and light. The monitor style appears almost exclusively in central Vermont, some of the eastern central seaboard states, and in central California's agricultural valleys south of Sacramento.

Double Dutch barn, Ellis farm, Springfield Township, Michigan
Norman Ellis was a livestock broker, buying and selling herds from all over the county. Ellis met a builder who enlarged existing plans to build him a barn suitable to house herds in transit. Ellis got interested in breeding and training Percherons, and the barn got a ground-floor 33x83-foot arena.

Similar to the earlier New England connected barns, all functions were to be housed under one roof for convenience and efficient operation. The barn front wall and milking parlor faced the house, barely 100 feet away. The long side wing on the north was an enormous milking parlor. Above these was feed storage. The south wing was originally the horse barn, and hay was stored above that as well. A wing at the rear, parallel to the front milking room, held calf pens. Other than through wide doorways to the horse barn, interior access on the ground level was uninterrupted. The haymow above it all was continuous. This was as close as possible to a production-line dairy operation.

Located in the center of this C-shaped complex was the small breeding barn.

The barn, constructed of jack pine that Fancher had hauled up from the South, measured more than 144 feet across the front, while the longest wall—the north one—was nearly 210 feet. The top of the roof measured 40 feet from the ground. The cupola and its weather vane rod—a hand-hammered, copper, life-size cow—added another 20 feet to the overall height.

Norman Glen Ellis was another very successful stock trader and broker who dealt in sheep, cattle, and horses. Based in Michigan, he brought home not only livestock from his road trips but ideas as well.

Ellis' working technique was to buy and sell while on the road. He traveled constantly throughout the Midwest and the Northeast. Whatever stock he acquired remained at the farm where he bought it until its new owners arranged for pick up. Ellis built a large, elegant home for his wife in the mid-1880s. When it was complete, it dwarfed his small barn. With only a few Percheron horses at home, he had no real reason to have a large barn. Nonetheless, his friends and neighbors began to tease him about the big house, big success, and tiny barn.

After nearly a year of enduring this, Ellis met a barn builder named Brock. Ellis saw some examples of his work and he liked the appearance and the quality of the structures. They talked and Ellis ordered a barn to be built for him in Michigan.

The barn, best described as a Madawaska Twin Barn, is a style that is found, though on a much smaller scale than Ellis version, in far northern Maine and even up into Quebec. Ellis' barn measured more than 56 feet from front to back and nearly 129 feet across the front, not including the double stallion shed built outside to keep them away from the mares. From the ground to the roof peak was just shy of 48 feet. Included in the barn on the ground floor is an 82x34-foot indoor riding ring. Eleven spacious box stalls also helped fill the ground floor, along with tack rooms, an office, and in the far corner, a mechanical exercise ring.

It is easy to think that life was crude and simple more than 100 years ago, to forget that barns were becoming factories to produce milk and beef, and mechanization was already taking the place of manpower in the routine exercise of race and show horses. In the late 1800s, the world was already beginning to shrink.

Inside the 56x129-foot double Dutch, or Madawaska Twin barn, builder Brock and owner Ellis wanted enormous hay storage capacity. The roof soars 47 feet above the haymow floor. With such a large freespan, the building flexed under the load of hundreds of tons of hay. The builder included bolted tuning beams that held in the sidewalls when the haymow was full.

67

CHAPTER 7

REBIRTH OF THE BARN

The year 1900 began not only the Century of Electricity, but it was also the start of a new era of science, research, and hygiene. Chemists looked into the wholesomeness and purity of milk and found bacteria and dust in wood barns. Scientists inaugurated elaborate procedures. They told farmers to clean and groom their cows one hour before milking to remove barnyard filth and loose animal hair. An hour, they reasoned, was long enough to let the freshly stirred dust settle inside the barn and for the cows to calm themselves.

Dairy barn, Beresford, British Columbia
Ideas moved across country in the minds of the settlers. This New England-style gable-end-entry dairy barn featured a gambrel (bent leg) roof yet it was constructed in the early 1920s of hand-hewn timbers adzed to fit. Builder Joseph Giacomuzi abandoned this 26x32-foot barn in the early 1940s when British Columbia prohibited milking dairy cows on wood floors for sanitary reasons.

Brick dairy barn, Petramala farm, Trinidad, Colorado
Built around 1910 from a plan for a New England barn from Pennsylvania, the owners used native materials to construct their 36x172-foot barn. Southeastern Colorado soil produces better clay than wood, although interior framing is of fir, the only wood available from nearby mountains.

When Albert and Madeline Petramala acquired the farm in 1945, Colorado had just changed sanitation laws to prohibit milking on wood floors. The Petramalas tore out the wood and rebuilt the long parlor using plaster of Paris. Petramala and his crew milked 440 Guernseys, 82 cows at a time, twice a day.

During that hour, the farmer was to disrobe, shower, and scrub thoroughly, and then dress again in fresh, clean milking clothes. Only after the last cow was milked, the last drop of milk stored safely and securely (and the farmer had changed back from the "milk" clothes into the "barn" clothes) could the herd be fed its dusty, dirty, insect-ridden meal of hay and grain.

This lengthy ritual made sense to a growing population of city dwellers, but it would take state and federal legislators to enforce what common sense—and the scientists—were saying should be done to protect milk drawn by hand into open buckets. In the meantime, farm and agricultural journal writers and magazine editors joined architects who had begun to discuss and consider on paper some solutions to the problems of sanitation.

In his 1913 book *Modern Farm Buildings*, professional architect Alfred Hopkins argued that, to ensure certification for the farmer's milk, a separate milk room should exist. "The real reason for this room," he wrote, was "to provide a place that may be kept free from flies, odors and dust." Hopkins text overturned practices that had been universally accepted for hundreds of years. Each formerly standard procedure was now dismissed as unhealthful.

The results of all this scientific discovery and architectural reasoning was a flurry of legislation that issued strict rules—and created new expenses—for farmers who sought to sell their milk to the public. In some regions, these kinds of costly modifications came as one more nail driven into the coffin of small farming. Their effects on New England's often struggling small farm operators were devastating. Many

Horse barn, Meadowfarm, Orange, Virginia
The crown jewel of Sears Roebuck's mail order barn catalog was this Sylvania stable. Stretching 210 feet long and 54 feet wide, it contains 18 stalls and uses 2,273 panes of glass to brighten the interior. Sears shipped such "kits" as this on flatbed rail cars from Chicago or New Jersey, and construction crews could be ordered as well to assemble the barn on site.

of them were already working at barely subsistence-farming levels. They got by only through a myriad of small home industries. The costs of updating their barns to new local, state, and federal hygiene standards brought a large number of New England farmers to their knees.

Large-scale industry wasn't finished with America's farmers and barns. The development and popularization of the hay baler put an architectural and engineering burden on century-old barns. These machines reduced the bulk of loose hay by nearly two-thirds. A ton of loose hay took up nearly 500 cubic feet, and this was one reason that the haymows assumed the proportions they did. A ton of baled hay occupied only 150 cubic feet, spreading the same load on a much smaller floor area.

After years of neglect, barns finally began receiving attention from architects at the beginning of the twentieth century.

Framing is yellow pine. The Sylvania boasts a 14-foot-wide exercise ring around its perimeter. A tack room and luxurious office were included on either side of its main cross aisle. Sears began selling building materials in 1895 and it introduced mail order buildings in 1909, offering houses, barns, granaries, garages, and shops for town and country.

Perhaps the most celebrated architect to design barns was Frank Lloyd Wright. Located near Spring Green, Wisconsin, Wright's barns were part of a complex that the architect designed for himself. It was meant to be not only his residence and design studio but also a working farm. He called the residence "Taliesin," after a Welsh poet whose name meant "the shining brow."

Eventually the Taliesin property grew to nearly 600 acres and included a site he selected for new farm buildings, a complex he called Midway Farm. The highest barn of the complex was the chicken coop, built as a bridge between the round hill and the top of the dairy cow barn. At the end of the dairy barn, but in what was the center of the farm building complex, he built a round tower, a stone turret of limestone with a hexagonal array of windows just beneath a hipped roof.

Wright's deeply held belief was that each building, no matter what its purpose, had dignity. It makes sense then that the same thought and attention—and passion—that he gave to each client and each commission, Frank Lloyd Wright also gave to his own barns.

Almost diametrically opposed to what Frank Lloyd Wright sought to accomplish with his highly individualistic

Sears Roebuck kit dairy barn, Meadowfarm, Orange, Virginia
Sears' mail order dairy and horse barns were available in widths from 24 to 40 feet and in almost any length. The structures were well designed with haymow floor joists of doubled yellow pine 2x10s on 18-inch centers. This barn measured 37x70 feet.

architecture was what mail order giants Sears Roebuck, Montgomery Ward, and others achieved through their catalogs. Starting probably around 1905 and continuing until the 1940s, barns were available by mail order, precut, ready to build, and delivered to the purchaser's site. These barns fulfilled the ever-growing number of legal and scientific requirements of the day.

As early as 1895, the Sears catalog included building materials for barns. In its 1911 "Book of Modern Homes," Sears offered four barn models. The most reasonable was Barn No. 11 at $377. This was an English-style barn designed to accommodate three cows, a calving pen, and four horses. It measured 26x46 feet. At the high end, Barn No. 14 sold for $792. It was nearly 40x70 feet and would accommodate seven milking stalls, eight horse stalls, and a 14x40-foot sheep stable.

"For $792," its literature explained, "we will furnish all the material to build this Barn, consisting of Rough Lumber, Heavy Framing Timbers, Plank Flooring, Shingles, Sash, Hardwood and Paint, Hay Carrier, Track and Rope. By allowing a fair price for labor and concrete blocks, which we do not furnish, this barn can be built for about $1,250, including all material and labor." Another $56 bought the farmer a 16x26-foot, 12-foot-tall, lean to shed that could be attached to the sheep stable's long wall. Paint was furnished in the buyer's choice of color, and the shipment provided enough to yield two coats. Three of the four designs in the catalog were topped off with the new, popular gambrel roof style, while the large No. 14 barn was available only with an ordinary steep-pitch gable roof.

The 1916 catalog introduced Barn No. 65, an octagonal dairy barn 54 feet across. For $749, the farmer got plans and materials to build the barn—including "Sea Green Slate surfaced roofing." For another $1.50, plans were also available for a chicken house, hog house, machinery and tool shed, corn crib, and silo.

"This is an octagon barn," Sears catalog writers claimed, "of first class construction and is becoming very popular throughout the country. Our floor plans afford an economical arrangement. There are stalls for twenty-four cows, a box stall, calf pens, and room for a silo in the center. We will furnish the material for the silo for $157.00 extra."

In 1918 Sears published *The Book of Barns—Honor-Bilt-Already Cut.* On its front and back covers were gothic

The most popular roof design was this Gothic arch truss style. Sears used balloon frame construction for economy and ease of construction, with sandwiches of 2x8s bolted together, soaked, bent, permanently warped, and then laminated into these graceful arcs. Making the roof start as a wall gave useful floorspace right to the edges of the structures.

Dairy barn, Taliesin North farm, Spring Green, Wisconsin
Architect-designed barns are quite uncommon throughout history. Especially rare is the attention of an internationally renowned designer to farming. But Frank Lloyd Wright called Taliesin North his farm and his students spent as much time working the earth as working at drawing boards on Prairie School structures that evolved from Wright's love of the land.

Livestock barn, North Head Lightstation, near Ilwaco, Washington
Designed by Lighthouse Board architect Carl Lieck, this 30x40-foot barn sat far inland from the windblown lighthouse, nestled behind the headkeeper's residence and a larger duplex built for the two assistant keepers. Lieck loosely based his design on the Mormon Cattle barn with its gable-on-hip-roof treatment. He flanked his haymow door with typical lighthouse residential quarter-round windows for light and ventilation.

arched-roof barns. Not only did Sears expand the architectural styles it included in its catalogs, but it also kept its architects and lumber millers busy designing and issuing specifications for each of its barns in a variety of widths and lengths. The "Cyclone Modern Barn," for example, was offered from 24x24 feet with "select Cyprus siding" for $550, growing in increments up to a 40x140-foot version with a haymow capable of 167-ton capacity for $3,484 with the same siding.

By comparison, Sears' largest timber-frame barn—also 40x140 feet—with its steep-pitched gable roof, was rated at a 266-ton haymow capacity. It sold for $3,407 when ordered with comparable materials. However, the 1918 catalog didn't stop there. Its octagonal barn had grown to 60 feet in diameter, 44 feet in height, and now had a hay capacity of 50 tons.

Sears introduced a 60-foot round barn of similar dimensions and capacity selling for $1,682.

In its 1929 barn catalog, Sears published several pages showing the differences in time and labor charges involved to construct a scratch-built barn compared to purchasing their precut ready-to-assemble barn of the same size. Measuring and cutting on the site, Sears claimed, added another 360 hours to what it took to assemble its barn.

Barns were shipped by one or more railroad boxcars from the yard in Cairo, Illinois, or Newark, New Jersey, to the nearest drop point, and then by truck or wagon to the farm. It was an early example of Just-In-Time inventory control: shipments were timed to arrive at about the point where the carpenters would be assumed ready for the next materials. Blueprints and construction manuals arrived before anything

Carl Lieck's stylish barn featured two lean-to additions. A wagon shed on the back nestles into the encroaching woods. A Swiss-style forebay on the front provides protection from the frequent Pacific northwest winter rain showers. The headkeeper's residence is in the background.

was shipped, with elevations, plans, and framing details included. Sears' own architects sometimes designed these barns, and starting in 1919, the company established an official design department called the Architectural Division.

Throughout the late 1920s, Sears had begun to carry a larger share of its customers' financial arrangements, in some cases financing the full cost of materials and construction through its liberal financing plans. When the Depression hit in October 1929, it caused Sears difficult times for the next several years as home owners and farmers struggled—or failed—to meet the payment terms and to survive. To make matters worse, Sears fell victim to a classic example of a good idea at a bad time. In 1929 the company began to offer its barns assembled on site by its own crews. While this provided a tremendous benefit and convenience to the buyer who no longer needed even to find a carpenter crew, it incorporated for Sears the factor of workers' wages as an additional element of its financial risk. By 1933, at the depths of the Depression's impact, Sears planned to discontinue Midwest sales of ready-to-build structures (and it did stop building them itself).

Sears' Modern Homes Department was disbanded in 1934 and by 1940 it was out of the business of selling precut, ready-to-assemble barns.

CHAPTER 8

RESURRECTION & PRESERVATION

Gil White slipped through the double doors out into the frosty, early morning April sunlight to feed the hogs. Barely a dozen animals, all 4-H projects, filled the yard. They squealed and grunted in delight at the arrival of breakfast. After he emptied each bucket load, Gil shoved open one of the 6.5x10-foot brilliant red doors, each trimmed and crossed in stark white.

Abandoned dairy barn, near Fargo, North Dakota
The future lies outside the past. Once silage equipment manufacturers such as New Holland perfected hay rollers, the need for barn storage of cattle feed decreased. These 1,400 to 2,200-pound hay rolls replaced 12 to 20 large bales, cutting human labor as well. These tight, dense rolls resisted moisture and no longer needed to be stored inside.

High-drive, banked barn, Samuel Randall farm, Huntington Center, Vermont

Vermont is a fascinating state to study barn development. Simple English barns were influenced by French immigrants from Canada, then Germans from Pennsylvania, and later by the Scots. By 1840, immigrants had been there for two generations and styles evolved into complex structures. Over the next 20 years, Yankee frugality simplified structures.

"Our great grandfather, William Cook, built this barn in 1917," White said. "It was his pride and joy. It takes a lot of work. But we knew what we had to do when it came time."

In 1995, Gil White and his brother, David, had to confront a hard decision. They had made a commitment to their family farm in St. John, Washington, completely taking over its day-to-day operation from their father during the winter of 1991–1992. Centerpiece of the farm was the large gothic arch truss barn.

St. John is wheat country and William Cook and later his son, Roy, farmed it with horses and mules, which they housed in the spacious, contemporary barn. In 1945, the

Cooks modernized their operation, selling the horses and switching over to tractors. They got rid of the loose hay in the 37-foot high haymow. In its place—and taking advantage of the vast, nearly unobstructed upper floor—they built a 9,000-bushel granary and an elevator inside the barn. The granary took care of what they needed for feed as well as their own seed requirements.

Roy Cook's son-in-law, Curtis White—David and Gil's father—took over in 1968 when Cook died. The Whites changed to a simpler feeder operation, but that market went bad several years later. In 1982, they got rid of the remainder of the cattle and the last of the horses they kept to work them.

Built in 1895, the 45x100-foot barn was an active dairy farm until 1986. Built against the hillside surrounding this valley, the barn began to slide on the clay soil once the warming effect of the cows inside was removed. In 1995, Sarah Williamson, an organic vegetable farmer, bought the property with its house and barn and began an extensive repair project, saving the barn from collapse.

Signed and dated, the builder and his crew were proud of their work. A century later, Sarah Williamson respects that pride and has invested considerably in preserving the hemlock and spruce wood barn. While an active dairy farm until 1986, the animals' body heat kept the ground below the barn from freezing. Since that time, frost heaves had shifted the barn toward the road, and the work to save the building was extensive.

The farm grew. They continued to fill the barn granary each fall. But other silos on the farm were easier to load and empty.

Curtis White began to turn over the farm and its operation to Gil and David in 1987. The transition was complete four years later and the sons quickly came face to face with their dilemma.

"The barn had become almost useless," David White explained. "We didn't have horses, or mules, or the cow-calf operation. The barn needed to be painted, and needed a roof!"

The wood barn's north and south gable ends stood 47 feet, 6 inches to the peak, and they were 45 feet, 10 inches across. The long walls—76 feet, 4 inches long—were 11 feet to the eaves on the east, shorter on the west because of the hillside. By the time all the restoration work was done

in 1995, that wood had consumed 84 gallons of red and 10 more gallons of white paint. It took 6,000 shingles to do the roof.

"Well," David said, "there was really no question. It's a part of our history. We're the fourth generation on this farm, the fourth generation to look out our windows and see that barn every day. There was just no question that we'd repaint it, repair the roof. I mean, what else would we do? Tear it down?"

Far across the country, Sarah Williamson faced a much larger problem with equal resolve. Williamson, an organic vegetable grower in Huntington Center, Vermont, went looking for a farm. She found a modest 20-acre site with a lovely 165-year-old brick home and, across the road, a huge high-drive bank barn that was sliding down the hill.

Dairy barn, southern Ohio
Barn advertising is only as permanent as paint on wood. Until Harley Warrick's death in early 2001, Mail Pouch's (and probably America's) most prolific barn painter occasionally came out of retirement to touch up a barn for friends. Depending on the weather, ads depicting tobacco, soft drinks, and tourist destinations last barely five years before they fade from view and into memory.

In 1895 Samuel Randall hired a crew to construct the barn with its high center drive, its tall cupola, and its covered-bridge entry ramp. He told anyone who'd listen, that he was building a barn for his grandchildren. Randall built it with access to their high field across the road, banking the barn against the blue-clay hillside facing his house.

The barn went out of active dairy farming in the early 1980s. The body heat of the cows and insulation that their manure provided through the long winters disappeared; the frosts and thaws began to move the huge barn. When Sarah bought the place, she found Duncan Keir, a Vermont native who ran a business called Liberty Head Post and Beam. Sarah Williamson told him, "This barn is 100 years old. I want it fixed so it will last another 100 years."

The barn was well built, but the foundation was just indigenous river rock that was held together with lime mortar. That mortar probably deteriorated within the first 40 years, according to Keir. The barn basically sat on loose rock and was sliding toward the road.

Throughout the winter of 1995–1996, Keir and his crew worked to straighten the barn, a delicate and costly procedure. By spring, the crew had raised the ramp 2.5 feet and, using six 2-ton block-and-tackles, they pulled the posts within an inch of vertical again.

Through the spring of 1996, Keir and his crew lifted the entire building off the ground, excavated for a new footing well below the frost line, and poured concrete to ground level. They let that set and harden, and then rebuilt the stone

Monitor barn, Venture Farm, Winooski Valley, Vermont
Moses and Uziel Whitcomb, third owners of the farm, built the 55x110-foot barn in 1901 as they expanded its original 330 acres to nearly 1,000. The barn uses a monitor-style New England gable roof. This is basically a cupola that is stretched to the entire length of the roof, offering much greater air ventilation and light than one or more traditional cupolas.

foundation. By November they had lowered the barn, securing it to its new base.

"This is an act of faith," Sarah Williamson said, looking again at her barn. "I don't have the confidence that previous owners had that my grandchildren will live here. When this barn was built, that was expected. These things were built with structural integrity. They'll be here for generations. And what I'm doing is just making sure that this one will be here, too."

During the spring of 1996, the state of Vermont adopted a similar attitude with respect to a pair of large monitor-roof barns built in the same high-drive style as Sarah Williamson's, both in need of extensive repair.

William Freeman established the farm on which these barns are located in 1851. Freeman accumulated about 330 acres and then built a modest barn near the road. In 1854 he sold the farm to M. S. Manwell who turned the place into a dairy farm. In 1871, Uziel Whitcomb and his son Moses bought it.

The Whitcombs built a carriage barn in 1900 and followed that in 1901 with the 55x110-foot, four-story dairy barn with its monitor-type roof. In 1904, they added a second monitor barn, of 45x90 feet, several hundred yards west of the first one. But during the Depression, Moses Whitcomb's outside investments failed and he lost the farm to the bank.

Not only does air and light come in through loosely spaced siding planks on the monitor, but this barn also directs fresh air downward through the wooden boxed airshafts. Monitor barns are uncommon. They seem to have originated in this valley, migrated to central Virginia and then far west to the central agricultural valleys of California, truly ideas carried not in magazines or blueprints but in the minds of settlers and immigrants.

In 1948, Xenophon Wheeler acquired the property and renamed it the Venture Farm. In the early 1950s, he remodeled the manure sink in the barn basement to meet federal and state health and sanitation regulations. He poured a concrete floor and set up a free-stall milking parlor. By the 1960s Venture Farm was producing 6,000 pounds of milk a day. Wheeler added two milking sheds onto the west side of the big monitor barn in the early 1970s. When he retired, he sold the farm to a succession of owners each of whom proved incapable of running the place profitably. Holding the mortgage himself, he continued to own the place until finally, in 1983, he threw in the towel. No qualified buyers could be found in the shaky economy. Venture Farm was withdrawn from active use. Various plots of land were sold off until May

1994, when the Vermont Farm Bureau purchased the remaining 170-acre farm with its house, smaller barns, and the large monitor barn.

The smaller barn had lost many of its green slate roof tiles. There was serious internal structural damage from moisture. The large barn, its slate roof intact, had lost only a small area of second floor wall at the southeast corner. The covered bridge ramp up to the high drive had been removed, and the west-side dairy shed additions were gone.

Venture Farm was listed on the National Register of Historic Places in 1994. The Farm Bureau had a number of plans it was considering for future uses of the barn.

The Depression that took Moses Whitcomb out of large-scale farming dashed the aspirations of an Ohioan as well. However, while Whitcomb had been at it for nearly three decades and had built two large barns at a sensible and practical pace, Frederick Widder's ambitions had a monumental scale to them.

Widder had made a fortune in steel, but his personal life revolved around horses, and his profitable steel operations allowed him to indulge a fantasy. So in mid-1927, Widder purchased nearly 370 acres of farmland and designed a barn to house what he decided would be the finest—and largest—horse-breeding operation in Ohio, if not the United States. He met with architects and engineers who teamed up to design for him a barn large enough to house 250 to 300 horses and their feed through a long, snowy winter.

It would be built with wood, but not of wood, however. Widder didn't know wood. He knew steel and this barn would be a steel truss building. In early 1928, he obtained a mortgage for $23,000, pledging as collateral the land he'd bought. In late summer of 1929, with construction under way, he set off to buy horses while a crew of big-city steel workers constructed his 101-foot–wide, 202-foot-long, clear-span steel barn. When it was finished, it would stand 60 feet tall.

But Widder's timing in this case was not so good, and his barn never housed the huge herds of America's finest horse-breeding stock, because on Tuesday, October 29, 1929, Widder lost all of his money in the stock market. By August 20, 1932, the property was in tax delinquency.

Nearly 70 years have passed since Frederick Widder had the idea to build his giant, steel-truss, clear-span barn. Had he lived, he would have seen that he had invented the future of the barn. His idea was not farfetched; he merely had too big an idea too soon.

Monitor cattle barn, northwest of Hanford, California
This blending of Vermont monitor barn and Mormon Cattle barn is unique to a narrow region in central California, a searingly hot area in the summer. Its low eaves turn back hard winds yet the open monitor at the peak of the roof encourages air flow to dry hay and other cattle feed.

This open-ventilation roof style dispels summer temperatures that can reach 115 degrees in August and September and may be the principal reason this style landed in Central California on otherwise square western, or Mormon cattle barn-style structures. This barn measures 48x44, and at its peak reaches 28 feet.

Cattle bank barn, Odenkirk farm, Orrville, Ohio
A traditional New England banked barn this is not. Steel magnate Fred Widder built it in 1928, with the ambition of breeding horses. He designed a structure large enough to winter 600 head. Steel technology would handle it. The 101x202-foot barn roof is supported by bridge-size trusses 12x60-feet, offering 20,000 square feet of open haymow with cattle pens below. The barn is 60 feet tall.

In Kansas City, Missouri, the Butler Manufacturing Company has been producing what it called "pre-engineered metal buildings" since before the 1920s. These began with a simple 10x17-foot one-car garage fabricated out of the same corrugated steel that Butler used for its round grain bins.

Pre-engineering, to Butler, meant prefabricated, with all the stress and load-bearing considerations done mathematically on paper prior to mass production. By the early 1940s, Butler offered a complete line of rigid frame buildings.

The company provided thousands of these structures under military contract to the U.S. government during World War II. When the war ended, with Butler's production still at wartime levels, the company simply sold off its excess as "military surplus" buildings. The civilian population had been asked to do without nearly everything during the war and when it ended, both agriculture and industry found intense need for buildings in a great hurry. Butler sold thousands of the war surplus stock and established an

Gothic arch truss cattle barn, White farm, St. John, Washington
Built in 1917, this barn evolved from housing a cow/calf breeding operation to a 9,000-bushel-capacity granary feed facility in the former haymow, begun in 1945. The family still farms for seed but most of its equipment is too large to move in or out of the 46x76-foot barn.

international reputation, first for the quality of its product and second for its willingness to adapt its standard buildings to its customers' specific needs. Doors could be made wider and taller. Roofs could be raised to accommodate the largest harvesters or any piece of specialized equipment. As Sears had done a decade earlier with its wooden barns, now Butler did with its steel buildings. A crew showed up with the materials and built the shed or barn on the farmer's site in a fraction of the time it would take for timber frame construction. What's more, it cost less than the wood barn. And a new roof meant nothing more than simply unrolling another sheet of corrugated steel and riveting it into place.

By the 1950s, Butler's rigid frame, pre-engineered steel buildings—and the company's national and regional competitors—had turned the wood barn into an expensive anachronism. Steel went up in a week at most, and there was

nothing that wouldn't fit inside. Technology had put wood barns on notice. And technology wasn't finished.

In the mid-1970s, farm equipment manufacturers moved beyond the hay bailer and perfected hay rollers. These machines grabbed sixteen bales worth of wind-rowed hay and rolled it into a weather-shedding, airtight drum that could be left in fields for months, seasons, a year or more, without appreciable degradation of the hay just below the surface.

Technology brought plastic wrap to farm fields. Implement designers conceived of the machinery to shrink-wrap individual rolls of hay, keeping out mice, rats, insects, and mold. Who needs barns anymore?

Throughout the history of the barn in the New World, there have been dozens of factors that have contributed to its demise.

One such factor was a property tax system that penalized farmers for routine maintenance. Investing $5,000 or $10,000 in a new roof or a coat of paint to protect a barn from the

Even though it's been 20 years since the White family bred cattle, and half that since the feed and seed operation outgrew the building, the family has made serious commitments to preserve the barn, painting and reshingling it in 1995. With nearly 3,000 acres of winter wheat and spring barley, the family now uses the barn primarily as home for a few 4-H hog projects.

elements or to keep the structure sound resulted in a visit from the local tax assessor. The assessor rewarded the farmer for his preservation work with a tax increase since new shingles or paint was looked upon as an improvement to the property.

Sanitation laws that purified milk were certainly necessary. But the cost was beyond what many farmers could afford, and they simply quit farming. Huge barns that made sense during active dairy farming have become incredibly costly to repair when the only benefit is to the ambiance of the village or hillside.

The National Trust for Historic Preservation has helped. Established in 1949, it has marshaled ideas and

information and funds to form a variety of sources to protect and preserve agricultural buildings. A building may be designated as a historic landmark or listed in the National Register of Historic Places, and its owners are then eligible to take a 20 percent income tax credit on the cost of rehabilitating such buildings.

John Walter, conservation editor of *Successful Farming* magazine, invented a program in 1987 to preserve historic farm buildings. Farmers could receive financial rewards for their born-again barns. The program, BARN AGAIN, has helped hundreds of active farmers repair, renovate, remodel, reactivate, and reuse their aging—and sometimes

Livestock barn, Point Sur Lightstation, Big Sur, California
Living atop the 360-foot-high rock called Point Sur Lightstation was a special challenge. High winds required the keepers to tether their cows and chickens to keep them from blowing off the rock. The small barn sits near the middle of the 1,000-foot-long rock, near where keepers raised small plots of vegetables.

ailing—barns. The program's goal is to keep the structures not only standing but also functioning efficiently.

Out in tiny Bruno, Nebraska, Herman Ostry bought a farm a half-mile out of town. A 28-foot-square barn came with the property. But when the creek rose in the spring, the floor of the barn disappeared under 29 inches of water. Every time it rained the barn got wet. There was always mud in it. Ostry could use only the haymow for storage.

At dinner one night after flood crest, Ostry bet that if enough people got together, they could just carry the barn up a nearby hill. There was laughter around the table. However, within a few days, Ostry's son Mike showed up with some calculations. He figured that the barn weighted 16,640 pounds. How much weight could an average person lift?

Bruno was planning to celebrate its centennial in late July. The organizers listened to Herman and Mike's idea and publicized that, as part of the celebration, there would be a barn raising.

"When 4,000 people showed up from 11 states, only a few were surprised by what the centennial committee had in mind," Herman Ostry recalled eight years later. "Mike had fitted 3,800 feet of 3/4-inch steel tubing through the barn to make handles for people to carry it.

"Everybody lifted up the barn, turned the front wall from the east to the south. They moved it 115 feet south and about 6 feet up the gentle slope. Three minutes after they raised the barn, they set it back down.

"It worked fine. And it saved the barn."

93

The small 20x30-foot barn faced away from strong prevailing north and west winds. After the original blew off the rock in a storm, a local volunteer organization rebuilt it. Lighthouses generally kept a cow or two for milk, and a horse or two for wagon rides into the nearest city. From Point Sur, Monterey was a day's ride each way in 1889 when the light was first activated.

Index

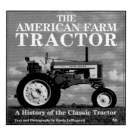
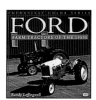
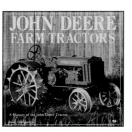
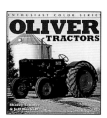